THE YOGA *of* MONEY MANIFESTO

A Radical New Way to Connect Your Mind, Body, Spirit, and Bank Account

EDWARD VILGA

"When I was young I thought that money
was the most important thing in life;
now that I am old I know that it is."
~ Oscar Wilde

Contents

INTRODUCTION:
RISING FROM THE MUD...

"No mud, no lotus."

~ Thich Nhat Hanh

PRACTICE VS. PROBLEM-SOLVING

Everyone from Thich Nhat Hanh to Goldie Hawn has noted that the Lotus is considered the most beautiful flower...and yet it only grows out of the mud.

Originating in the muck and mire, the lotus rises to the surface; only then does it gradually open its petals and reveal its glories as it blossoms in the sun.

This book—like much of my early financial life—definitely grows out of the mud.

You see, although I've been touted as "a legendary yoga master" by Bloomingdale's in the *New York Times* and included in *Yoga Journal*'s cover story about America's leading teachers, for much of my past I hardly ever experienced a consistent, Zen-like peace on the topic of money. Instead, there's been an abundance of contrast around the subject.

I'm the first person in my family to go to college (and I got myself into and through Yale despite my family's blue collar resistance).

I've taught yoga to billionaires while worrying about paying my cell phone bill.

I've raised over several million dollars for my own creative projects and can only imagine how many millions in budgets I've successfully overseen, though budgeting my own money has often been a mighty challenge.

I've been on a dozen TV shows and featured in 50+ publications including Oprah's *O Magazine*, *People*, *Cosmopolitan*, and even *Woman's World*, yet I am no stranger to worrying about the rent.

Twenty years ago, I married and divorced an heiress, choosing to walk away penniless, later to declare bankruptcy.

I've had my bohemian splendor loft life featured in an 8-page spread in *The Modern Estate*, an upscale shelter magazine, while battling my landlord in court.

I've even made a feature film centered around debt collection, starring Paul Sorvino and Justin Theroux entitled *DEAD BROKE* (Warner Brothers DVD, 2006), that won festival awards yet lost me a small fortune.

In short, I'm quite familiar with the mud.

Flashback…It's almost a decade ago, and I find myself adrift somewhere off New Zealand in the Tasman Sea.

My dearest friend has gifted me with a deluxe New Age cruise where every day at a seminar we hear an encouraging message that's basically "Don't Worry, Be Happy."

Meanwhile, my main source of income—virtually managing another best friend's yoga center—has dried up since she's unexpectedly about to close her doors. Sadly, there will be no direct deposit this month. I'm somewhere between Australia and New Zealand and I'm not sure if my rent check will clear.

Worse still, given the extremely limited TV that's available shipboard, I'm pretty much forced to watch Suze Orman confront yet another phone-in caller about his foolish choices. Wise mentor—even financial savior to some—Suze makes me grind my teeth. In fact, right now she seems particularly delighted to fuel my feelings of confusion and near despair (although I do enjoy wondering if detailing the unique complexities of my situation would make her head explode on camera).

As Suze berates person after person with her "scared straight schtick" for their financial foibles, I recall the 16th century Sufi mystic Hafiz who counters her kind of adamant snap judgments with "Always Remember: Everyone is trudging along with as much dignity, courage, and style as they possibly can."

There's just got to be something other than these two extremes, I ponder, fully aware of the irony as I sip my complimentary champagne and worry about my plummeting bank balances.

Over the many years since then, as I dove deeper and deeper into my personal mud trying to master the topic of Money, I eventually achieved the career success and more and more of the financial peace I sought.

In my explorations, I discovered something surprising. There were two distinct conversations around the topic of money: the metaphysical/

mindset approach and the practical/number-crunching/materialistic camp.

I was first drawn to the metaphysical/mindset school of thought, the one which offers such classics as THINK AND GROW RICH by Napoleon Hill, CREATIVE VISUALIZATION by Shakti Gawain, ASK AND IT IS GIVEN by Abraham-Hicks, or any of the works by Deepak Chopra, particularly THE 7 SPIRITUAL LAWS OF SUCCESS.

Yet I also devoured books from the opposite camp, those with practical, checkbook-balancing, Roth IRA, FICO score kinds of information. Tomes such as THE MONEY BOOK: YOUNG, FABULOUS, AND BROKE by Suze Orman, or Andrew Tobias' THE ONLY INVESTMENT GUIDE YOU'LL EVER NEED, Dave Ramsey's TOTAL MONEY MAKEOVER, or Ramit Sethi's I WILL TEACH YOU TO BE RICH come to mind.

And yet...something was missing.

Or, more accurately, something was just not connected.

One of the most powerful and unique aspects of yoga is that it's a HOLISTIC practice.

Yoga is a combination of physical poses, meditation, and spiritual philosophy.

In fact, the word "yoga" literally means "union" in Sanskrit. That's because our goal is to connect Mind, Body, and Spirit, letting us plug into something greater than ourselves.

We don't do poses merely to achieve a "yoga butt" or tone our abs, but to release the body's tension so that we can calm our minds and explore our true nature. Yoga meets us where we are as humans, in both the material and spiritual realms.

The same could not be less true for all of the money books I could find. The approaches were so different, it was almost as though the authors were writing on entirely separate subjects. Recalling the classic story of three blind men fighting over their individual descriptions of an animal that turns out to be an elephant, there just wasn't any book where I could find a holistic approach.

I soon realized that all of the books viewed money through a mode of thought that's completely different from the one I experience in yoga. Whether New Age easy-breezy or Accountant-Friendly and spreadsheet ready, they are all about Problem Solving. The cornerstone of yoga, however, is that it is a *Practice.*

Seemingly similar, Practice and Problem Solving are actually radically different modes of thought.

For example, when we're solving a problem we're either future or past focused; we want to correct a mistake that's been made or prevent a future one from occurring. If we're engaged in Practice while we are immersed in corrective and preventative activities, we're actually centered in the present; our focus is on our experience of the here and now.

In Problem Solving mode, the reward is the Solution. In Practice, we achieve the necessary solution but the real reward is Self-Discovery.

Problem Solving really only values success. That's why most money experts treat past financial difficulties as failures that we should quickly recover from and avoid at all costs. In yoga, however, we often say that our injuries are our greatest teachers.

Furthermore, in Problem Solving mode we might seek out the answers from those experts, but in a Practice we know that deep down the real guru is within. That's why the first step in any Practice is

Self-Acceptance; with most Problem Solving financial gurus, in my opinion, unfortunately it's Shame.

Problem Solving is incredibly normative whereas Practice is extraordinarily personal. As a yoga teacher, I'm keenly aware of just how personal a yoga practice needs to be. I offer countless adjustments and variations, realizing that no two bodies are exactly alike. Nonetheless, cookie-cutter financial solutions are constantly offered via two-minute sound bites by on-camera money experts.

A final distinction is that Problem Solving is only needed until a solution has been found, whether that's getting out of debt or saving up for retirement. A Practice, on the other hand, is a life-long adventure, one in which even after achieving the necessary "solution," one is still continuously learning and growing.

Not one of these authors conceives money as a Practice...just a Problem to be solved, whether by mindset/metaphysics or switching accountants.

I began to wonder if perhaps I were truly on to something, if I had discovered a Practice for myself that might benefit others, and if the time was right to begin sharing it.

Going further in my exploration, I interviewed more than 50 people who were self-identified as yogis, meditators, or connoisseurs of spiritual/ wellness/self-improvement books, asking them dozens of questions about their hopes, fears, and concerns about money. I also wanted to know if this holistic money material was "out there" and I just hadn't found it, or whether this was indeed a new, perhaps even radical paradigm.

Those conversations proved invaluable in many ways, particularly because when I described what I was doing at the end of each conversation, a majority of interviewees freely proclaimed, "I need your book!"

It was also clear that for many of them—educated and sophisticated in so many ways and aspects of their lives—there wasn't a financial primer that spoke to them from a platform of who they were as human beings and spiritual seekers. "Personal Finance for the Financially-Clueless" simply held no appeal. They needed something more than that.

Realizing there was no "Yoga of Money," no holistic approach that addressed both mindset AND material concerns, I set about creating ways to share the truths I was discovering.

"We teach what we need to learn and
write what we need to know."
~ Gloria Steinem

I taught the first *YOGA OF MONEY* workshop to a dozen students at Exhale in NYC—the leading upscale spa chain in the United States—eager to confirm that people were truly receptive to this new approach. It was an extraordinary experience, deeply informative on multiple levels. I was perhaps most excited to learn afterwards that, unbeknownst to me, two finance professionals were in the room and that each experienced a different breakthrough insight.

As I shaped everything I wanted to cover in the workshop, I was delighted to discover that the way I sequence a yoga class—the order in which I present different types of poses—was a natural fit for the material. That gave the workshop a feeling of an authentic yoga practice, even as we dove into the themes of *THE YOGA OF MONEY* throughout. Through each pose, written exercise, or meditation, this sequence gave us a chance to really explore every money practice concept in our Bodies, Minds, and Spirits. I've extended the same structure for the material in this book, framing each chapter around a pose and including some thought-provoking exercises as well as some practical, numbers-driven suggestions.

After this I created several online courses, mastermind groups, and even more workshops, assembling and refining the material for this book.

I'm now thrilled to offer the world a book designed to truly transform a major component of your life.

Just as with the physical yoga practice, I expect each reader to find his or her own best way to flow with this material. In general, though, I'd recommend reading the book straight through but then going back and taking more time on each chapter to really absorb the material.

It's also worth noting that this book isn't designed to "fix" your financial life in a narrow window.

Instead, *THE YOGA OF MONEY* is just like a regular yoga practice: if you attend classes once a month, very little change occurs. When you keep showing up regularly (even if it's not every day), positive change is inevitable.

That's why I also want to remind you to be patient with yourself throughout this process.

If your hamstrings and hips are tight as tree trunks from decades of marathon running, it's not a reasonable expectation that after one yoga class you will be able to execute a full split or get your foot behind your head.

In the same way, in almost every case, your current financial situation was not created overnight. It's unrealistic to think that you will be able to transform it instantaneously either.

On the other hand, I've witnessed countless miracles working with people where breakthroughs happened at all points in their journey. Sometimes a tiny piece of alignment information (like moving the chest a little further forward in an arm balance, for example), is all that's required for a Quantum Leap.

You may very well experience many of these as you read and re-read this book.

Ultimately, I am 100% certain that a Money Miracle is possible for you, but as we all know, Miracles usually resist our attempts to schedule them. Stay enthusiastic and committed, however, and they are sure to arrive at the perfect moment.

One final note: as the creator of *THE YOGA OF MONEY*, I know how powerful this work can be on so many levels. I also know that resistance ALWAYS comes up in life, especially as we're nearing our edge or approaching a possible breakthrough.

Sometimes it may take the form of suddenly finding ourselves distracted. You might have some major breakthroughs and find that you inexplicably put this book back on the shelf.

Alternatively, general impatience may come up ("Nothing is happening" and "Why is this taking so long!").

And, of course, even long-held fears and insecurities, some of which are practically "old friends" and others which are unnamed but lurking in the background, may materialize and offer their unhelpful advice. ("This is just the way it is for me" and "Things will never change.")

The poet Robert Frost wrote, "The best way out is always through" and I encourage you to Practice with that in mind. Use every tool that's offered (and feel free to modify or invent your own), and together we'll "breathe your way through" to the other side.

I know that a better relationship with your finances will have such an enormously positive impact on your life that I couldn't be more excited to guide you in your journey.

That said, let's now begin a Yoga AND a Financial Practice that can transform our Body, Mind, and Spirit—and also our Bank Accounts.

Edward Vilga

THE TWELVE GIFTS OF YOGA & MONEY

CONNECTION	SELF-ACCEPTANCE	GROUNDING
FOCUS	CENTERING	TRANSFORMATION
CHALLENGE	EXPANSION	RELAXATION
MINDFULNESS	SURRENDER	GRATITUDE

CHAPTER 1

CONNECTION

OM

"You are not a drop in the ocean.
You are the entire ocean in a drop."

~ Rumi

CHANTING OM •
RECONNECTING

Yoga classes almost always begin and end with the chanting of OM.

This simple activity clues us immediately into the fact that we are not participating in just another fitness modality. OM reminds us that we are about to explore the CONNECTION between Mind, Body, and Spirit on several levels.

First, OM re-connects us with ourselves. Making this sound draws our attention within. Chanting OM is not about singing in the usual sense and certainly no vocal talent is required. Somehow adding sound to our breath has a palpable and immediate effect on our nervous system. It quickly calms us, turning down the volume of the mental chatter that runs wild during much of our experience.

Second, OM connects us all together in the room as a group, uniting teacher and students with each other. Yes, we remain distinct individuals practicing on our separate mats, each with our own challenges and gifts, but at the same time, we're now ready to enjoy a collective, shared experience together.

Third, OM allows us to connect to something beyond ourselves, something nameless but cosmic. OM represents the primordial vibration, the background hum of the Universe. Chanting it is a way to tune into that frequency, reminding us that we are more than just busy people sneaking in a fitness class between meetings. Without any dogma or even any explanation, it's an opportunity for us to reconnect with our spiritual natures, however we define those to be.

Reestablishing these multiple layers of connection—ourselves, our community, the cosmos; inward, outward, and beyond—are an inherent part of the Yoga Practice, one which we will learn to extend to our Financial Practice as well.

Although it might sometimes seem like our financial life is separate from our spiritual and emotional lives, nothing could be further from the truth. In order to truly succeed financially, we have to reconnect with our inner selves, we must learn to LISTEN TO OUR HEARTS.

Lost in a cluttered world of texts and emails, our brains are increasingly working overtime to process a trillion pieces of information every minute, which often leads to us losing touch with messages from our heart. Fortunately, you'll see it's easy to restore that connection since it's never really severed, only ignored.

How vital is this connection? It's absolutely essential. Unless you are living your purpose and following your heart, the benefits of money become relatively meaningless. And, more to the point, following your true passion is almost always the most direct way to creating and sustaining wealth in your life. As the bestselling book *Do What You Love, The Money Will Follow* by Marsha Sinetar advocates, listening to your heart's messages is the best way to define and travel your life's path and achieve the financial success you desire.

Note: None of us remains connected and aligned all the time. I try to be very candid that although I'm an internationally celebrated yoga teacher and best-selling author, I freely admit to having experienced major disconnections with Spirit and Money in the past and even challenging moments today. I'm certainly not alone in this (and neither are you).

In fact, as I've taught this material to more and more people, I've re-confirmed my suspicions that money really is the Last Taboo. People are often more willing to discuss details of their sex lives than share any aspect of their finances. Interestingly, this reluctance extends to both financial problems and to financial success, to wealth and poverty.

For example, I have a colleague who tells people she lives off of freelance writing earnings rather than admit that she's been blessed with a large family inheritance. I'm not suggesting she offer her tax return to everyone she meets casually, but presenting a very inaccurate version of her financial reality has much to teach her (and us) about fear, guilt, and preconceptions around money.

In contrast to this, many portray their financial situations as much better than they really are, keeping up affluent appearances despite the chaos behind the facade. In my own life, there were moments decades ago where I chose not to share my money struggles with family and friends, stating that I was just fine, only later learning that there were greater resources than I realized that would have been offered to me during this crisis period.

In the coming chapters, we'll discuss further how many experience considerable shame around money, including the feeling of money being the root of all evil, filthy lucre, or just plain "unspiritual." The same nonsense is often applied to the body, itself, which is why beginning a class with OM reminds us that everything—our bodies and our cash flow—is, in fact, sacred.

After chanting OM, I always pause for a moment before launching into physical instruction. There's a sense of drama and anticipation this creates, the students knowing that we're about to start vigorously moving and shape-shifting together, but that's not why I do it. In those still moments, I breathe in and out deeply, reminding myself that I'm here not just to instruct physical poses, to teach meditation, or to preach an abstract philosophy.

Rather, I'm about to share the physical, mental, and spiritual harmoniously blended together, summarized by the levels of Connection OM provides. It's this holistic connection that allows us to transform all aspects of our lives, especially now our Bank Accounts.

INVITATIONS TO PRACTICE: MIND, BODY, and BANK ACCOUNT

Mind

As we begin our exploration of *THE YOGA OF MONEY*, I invite you to meditate on what money means to you in your life and experience. What are the beliefs you hold about money—both positive and negative? What thoughts and feelings lie just beneath your conscious awareness? What and/or who shaped your perspective?

As you begin all these *YOGA OF MONEY* practices, journaling might be a wonderful means to uncover and focus your thoughts and emotions. You might also consider partnering with a like-minded friend to explore more fully each concept, sharing your discoveries, and investigations through each chapter.

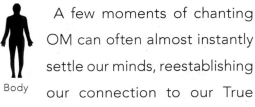
Body

A few moments of chanting OM can often almost instantly settle our minds, reestablishing our connection to our True Selves. Of course, this connection is ultimately unbreakable, but we can sometimes temporarily lose our awareness and mistakenly believe we've lost it forever.

If chanting feels too public or too foreign for you, simply consider watching your breath. Something as simple as lying down and placing one hand on your heart and another on your belly, focusing on how your lower hand rises up on the wave of the inhale and descends on the exhale, can powerfully draw your attention inward.

Alternatively, if chanting OM opens up new avenues for you, you could explore other more complicated mantras, particularly those geared towards increasing the energy of Abundance.

I've written about my favorite of these—
OM GUM SHRIM MAHA LAKSHMIYE NAMAHA—on my website, along with an accompanying audio meditation.

Devote some time to observing yourself whenever money comes into your experience in any way, particular through your personal spending and saving. What feelings and thoughts come up whenever you experience currency change hands? You might consider the exercise of tracking every penny in a notebook or a spreadsheet for a certain period, noting not only the amounts that come and go but also the feelings associated with each transaction.

Bank Account

CHAPTER 2

SELF-ACCEPTANCE

CHILD'S POSE

"Yoga is not about self-improvement
It is about self-acceptance."

~ Gurmukh

CHILD'S POSE •
LETTING GO OF SHAME

After OM-ing together, I begin every yoga class with the same questions and statements, always asking if anyone has any injuries I should know about, if there are any beginners in the room, and most importantly, offering a reminder that Child's Pose is always an option whenever a break is needed. Like a flight attendant's "We're about to take off" speech, this is the information I must relay in order to insure a safe journey for my students.

Child's Pose consists of letting the knees fall to the ground and then sending the hips back to the heels. Arms can be placed forward for a light stretch or left more passively by one's side.

Unlike teachers of fitness classes who motivate by frenzied cheerleading, although I always try to inspire and offer a challenging experience, I am not a drill sergeant demanding yet another set of push-ups or another sweat-inducing pose. Instead, I remind students to retreat and rest when needed because I want them to reconnect with the childlike concept of SELF-ACCEPTANCE.

Self-Acceptance means embracing one's own uniqueness, particularly one's injuries and vulnerabilities. Not every pose is for everyone, and a perfectly healthy workout for one person might be truly damaging for someone with certain injuries, or even, for example, a blessing like a healthy pregnancy. While I'm offering a group flow, we're not playing a game of "Edward Says"; modifications are encouraged and breaks can be taken as needed. There truly are no cookie cutter solutions, no "one size fits all" for a universal physical practice.

The ability to rest in Child's Pose highlights each person's uniqueness, underscoring why yoga is said to be non-competitive and non-judgmental.

There is no SHAME in a yoga practice, nor should there be in one's financial life. You are not a bad person because you have tight hamstrings or because you have gone seriously into debt. Even when we can pinpoint the cause—you've been running marathons for years without stretching beforehand, or you've made impulse purchases with naive optimism—we don't judge you, and more importantly, you shouldn't judge yourself for your physical struggles or for your finances.

Even so, the current of Shame runs so strong in our culture that in nearly every class, I'll assist a student in what is truly a difficult shape, only to have him or her tell me they're sorry when they fumble. "There's really nothing to be sorry about," I'll reply with a smile, hoping I can eventually soften their knee-jerk apologizing for their "imperfect" poses.

I've often struggled with this sense of Shame in my own financial life, most vividly when filling out the 45-page application for my building's condo board. It's a quirk in NYC's rental laws that one must be officially approved by a condo board even though they cannot refuse anyone the landlord has accepted. That is, it's a pure formality, yet still a set of hoops one must jump through. At the time, although enthusiastically approved by my landlord, my financial statement was not what I wanted it to be. I found myself uncomfortable sharing this information with a group of strangers, mostly because it did not include the accomplishments I was genuinely proud of. There were no spaces on the application to boast about the art I'd created or the students whose lives I'd transformed. Instead, it was just a list of assets and liabilities that created a financial picture I judged quite harshly. In many ways, I inflated it to be an unflattering and embarrassing summary of my entire life and character.

Many financial gurus deliberately cultivate a sense of Shame to secure their own power. Your bad decisions are either moral failures (buying a widescreen TV to impress your friends) or sins of ignorance. You are either self-indulgent or an idiot. Of course, your sense of being deficient means you need to turn to them for all the answers, creating a shame-based relationship with an inappropriate amount of perpetual dependence.

Another aspect of Child's Pose is its invitation to be childlike, reminding us to be at peace with where we are no matter what our chronological age. We might simply be a beginner in the financial realm and that's OK. Or we might have injuries in our lives (divorces, unemployment, bad investments, even bankruptcy) that we need to heal and forgive in order to find Self-Acceptance. Sometimes we might even need to release our family's multi-generational financial history so that we can stop acting from our grandmother's experience of the Great Depression in 1927, nearly 100 years ago.

That's why in every class I remind students that Child's Pose is always an option. All of us need the reminder that shame has no place in our Practice, Physical or Financial. We are where we are, and we are who we are; and both of those are more than OK. Struggling against this is like fighting a battle in quicksand. Only by allowing ourselves authentic Self-Acceptance can we truly begin our journey of Transformation.

INVITATIONS TO PRACTICE: MIND, BODY, and BANK ACCOUNT

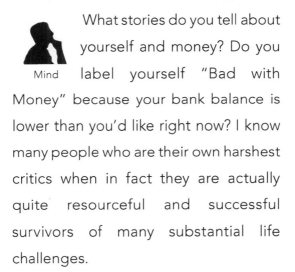

Mind

What stories do you tell about yourself and money? Do you label yourself "Bad with Money" because your bank balance is lower than you'd like right now? I know many people who are their own harshest critics when in fact they are actually quite resourceful and successful survivors of many substantial life challenges.

Do you have money secrets that even your closest friends, family, or partners do not know? Do you ever actively or passively present a false picture of your finances to the world?

In as compassionate a way as possible, explore how Shame affects your current financial life, knowing that healing it and moving forward freely is completely possible.

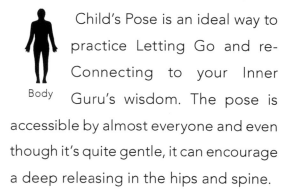
Body

Child's Pose is an ideal way to practice Letting Go and re-Connecting to your Inner Guru's wisdom. The pose is accessible by almost everyone and even though it's quite gentle, it can encourage a deep releasing in the hips and spine.

Of course there are many other ways you can explore feelings of release in the body and I encourage you to discover them. Massage is one as is taking a necessary nap. Frankly, any activity that allows you to withdraw your attention from your "Adult" dramas—perhaps flying a kite, driving a bumper car at an amusement park, or cuddling with a beloved pet—might also serve the same purpose.

What's most important is that you discover and continue to practice anything that allows you to release Shame or other negative emotions and return to the most Connected version of yourself.

Bank
Account

In the next chapter we will be diving deep into the numbers in our financial lives. For many, this might require some spring cleaning, even some detective work.

What systems do you have for tracking your finances and paying your bills? Should you invest in a computer program like Quicken? Are you a visual type who would turn this into a collage or craft project? Are all the figures you need readily available and at your fingertips or do you need to request documents or find items lost in your filing cabinet?

Or do you need to buy file folders just to get started?

As you do the physical preparation to look honestly at your numbers, explore the ways you can set this up that work best for you.

Don't forget that as you go deeper, new Mind/Body/Spirit/Bank Account conversations will arise internally. Remember that when these become stressful to always recommit to the practices of Self-Acceptance and Connection.

CHAPTER 3

GROUNDING

CAT / COW

"There are hundreds of ways to kneel and kiss the ground."

~ Rumi

WARMING UP •
KNOWING OUR NUMBERS

Cat/Cow Pose could not be more simple or more GROUNDING.

Kneeling on all fours, exhale as you tuck the tailbone down and let the head fall. Inhaling, tilt your tailbone and your gaze up, and enjoy opening your shoulders. Along with these two back and forth movements, I always invite students to move like themselves, allowing any wiggle or expressing any physical impulse to stretch.

Cat/Cow Pose is a perfect opening because I never start a yoga class with the most difficult pose that I'm going to teach. In fact, that would be more than a little crazy.

Instead, the first poses in a class are designed to both open the body in a gentle, gradual manner and also to draw the students' awareness to their physical selves in this present moment.

I always invite students to move like themselves, allowing any wiggle or expressing any physical impulse to stretch. I want them to "check in," as it were, with where they are Right Now, not where they were last week or even years ago. The body shifts day to day, and it is affected by everything from yesterday's intense workout or late night at the clubs, to a heavy breakfast, sleeping in an uncomfortable position, or a stressful work deadline. Even the weather on different days and the seasons themselves shift us physically. All of this can and should influence our yoga practice, but obviously that's only possible if we've taken the time to become self-aware.

In many ways, that's not only my first but also my primary job as a teacher: grounding my students in their own bodies so that they can pay attention to what they're actually experiencing inside themselves.

In the same way, when it comes to money, although it affects almost every aspect of our lives, a majority of people are often "checked out" about their finances. While a minority have a crystal clear notion of their assets and liabilities—knowing the interest rates on all their credit cards and the details of their 401K—others often have only a fuzzy notion related to their numbers, an assessment that doesn't go far beyond "I'm OK" or not. Most don't even really know what their monthly **NUT** is, the amount of money they need each month in order to get by.

Without physical or financial awareness, we're traveling blind, going through the motions but essentially adrift. We only "check back in" when an injury or a crisis suddenly demands our attention. Often, we're like patients afraid of the diagnosis but clearly aware we need medical treatment.

Putting this another way, in yoga there is no **OSTRICH POSE** where we stick our head in the sand, avoid reality, and just blindly hope everything works out!

Grounding ourselves requires getting a handle on our complete financial picture, an activity that will definitely draw once again upon the quality of Self-Acceptance we've been cultivating.

Just as in a yoga class we gradually warm up the body, so too we want our emergence into the objective reality of figures on a balance sheet to be gentle yet expansive, and most importantly, to keep our awareness grounded in present moment reality.

It is not necessary, nor is it helpful, however, for this process to be a Wake Up Call akin to being doused with an ice bucket of water. There is no "Band Aid of Financial Ignorance" that we're going to rip off as quickly as possible. Instead, we must find a way to ease our way into the experience. One way to achieve this is to approach our net worth from a holistic perspective.

Of course, you know deep down that you are infinitely more than any single set of statistics about yourself—weight, height, body fat, IQ, or in this case net worth—yet at the same time, since we are often our own harshest critics, we judge ourselves as successes or failures entirely based on our bank balances. When we're ready to open our credit card statements and become aware of the nuances of our APR, it's also important to keep remembering that we are not just a single cell Grand Total on an Excel spreadsheet.

Working organically, weaving back and forth between "getting real" with our numbers and appreciating other kinds of assets such as education, skills, achievements, relationships, and good health, can ease us through this scary process towards getting grounded and clear. More often than not, even if the situation is not ideal, it's rarely quite as bad as we thought it might be. In fact, there's usually a tremendous sense of relief once we know exactly where we stand.

Remember: Ostrich Pose is NOT ever going to work for you, but getting GROUNDED, staying CONNECTED, and SELF-ACCEPTANCE are the first steps in creating miracles.

INVITATIONS TO PRACTICE: MIND, BODY, and BANK ACCOUNT

Examine if you've been practicing Ostrich Pose

Mind around your money (or in any other important area of your life). Spend some time being honest with yourself in a non-judgmental way.

Remember that Ostrich pose might look very different for each individual. Whether it's secretly dreading upcoming financial events, ignoring a partner's spending, or indulging in any kind of external numbing behavior, whatever's beneath the surface is worth examining.

It's very important though that rather than condemning your Ostrich Pose and judging yourself harshly, that you soften and find compassion for the reasons why this might have been necessary. Unless we heal the reason you began avoiding your finances in the first place, it will be difficult not to make the same mistakes again.

Body

Cat/Cow is an excellent way to begin to warm up the body. Explore other simple stretches, for example a seated twist, a Happy Baby Pose, or even just a classic "Good Morning" stretch of lying down and reaching your hands above your head, fingers away from your toes.

Allow yourself to take inventory and to warm up the body (and examine your bank balances and financial statements) in a way that's gentle and exploratory, rather than rushed and unnecessarily demanding.

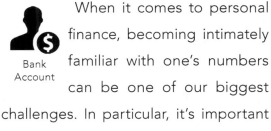

Bank
Account

When it comes to personal finance, becoming intimately familiar with one's numbers can be one of our biggest challenges. In particular, it's important that you understand and know your Monthly Nut.

Particularly if you've been practicing Ostrich Pose, these Grounding experiences may be challenging yet absolutely vital for your *YOGA OF MONEY* practice.

Remember that this doesn't all have to be done in one day and if it ever becomes overwhelming, you have Child's Pose and OMing to restore your sense of Connection and Self-Acceptance.

CHAPTER 4

FOCUS

WARRIOR POSE

"The successful warrior is the average
man, with laser-like focus."
~ Bruce Lee

STANDING POSES •
DREAMING AND GOAL SETTING

In the last three chapters, we've reconnected with ourselves, worked towards leaving our shame behind, and gotten grounded. We're now ready to really dive into creating the Financial Future of your Dream Destination.

Warmed up and self-aware, we're now ready for Warrior Poses, dynamic shapes which connect us to the powerful energy of our FOCUS. There are several Warrior Poses in the physical practice of yoga, highlighting the importance of taking a stand and connecting with our strength. The Warrior we reference, however, is a spiritual one, a hero without enemies (other than his or her own ego), who fights for true freedom.

Importantly, in Warrior Poses we gaze directly forward. We see what lies before us and determine where we want to go. The ability to make a strong and clear decision distinguishes the Warrior from the Victim, allowing us to travel a path of Aligned Action.

In our financial lives, having taken stock of where we are, it's now vital that we begin to determine our goals. Without them we are like rudderless ships, adrift at sea. Most of us, however, have never been trained in how to actually set goals (versus merely entertaining wishes and fantasies).

STEP ONE: DREAMING

The first step is that we have to allow ourselves to dream, to reconnect with what Martha Beck calls our "North Star." So many of us have become lost in the pragmatic, day-to-day issues of just getting by—did you know that 33% of the U.S. population is just one paycheck away from financial chaos—that dreaming may seem like an unaffordable indulgence. And yet if we are to have the life we really want—and the money to pay for it!—we must first reconnect with our true desires and aspirations.

In this chapter's INVITATION TO PRACTICE we remember what we've always loved (especially during our childhood) and to give ourselves permission to explore our secret, un-lived lives. We can rollick around with an "if there were no rules" mindset or "if money were no object" musings and see where those inquiries take us. Allowing yourself the freedom to simply dream and then look at your uncensored answers will enable you to see the common threads of what's most important to you, whether that's "more time with my family" or "a life of creative self-expression."

Refining and honing in on our priorities enables us to discover (and re-discover) what's behind the dreams that truly inspire us. For example, for some, Money will clearly mean Creative Freedom, while for others it might be Security, Family, Ease, or Relaxation. There is no "right answer" here, but the inquiry of uncovering the right answer for YOU is absolutely essential if your soon-to-be-defined financial goals are truly going to resonate and inspire.

STEP TWO: LEARNING HOW TO DEFINE OUR
GOALS

In *THE YOGA OF MONEY* we see our goals not exclusively as ends in themselves per se, but as ways of shaping our Practice. Nonetheless, we acknowledge that they are a key part of our journey.

Each chapter that follows this one explores distinct areas of our financial lives, ranging from Safety Nets to Retirement Planning. In each one, after fully diving into both the numbers and yoga-mindset components, we end with the opportunity for the reader to set appropriate, informed, and enlightened goals. Before we begin that journey, however, as Financial Warriors learning to Focus we must first truly understand what a goal is and what a goal is not.

Life coaches sometimes use acronyms when working with clients on goal setting. In *THE YOGA OF MONEY,* we'll work with (fittingly for Yoga) **MATS**. Our goals must fit the criterion of being **M**easurable,

Authentic, Time-Bound, and falling into the category I've labeled "Stretch." Allow me to further define each of our MATS elements.

First, our goals must be MEASURABLE. "Getting rich" is nebulous at best. Having that as a goal is akin to buying a plane ticket to "Some Undefined Northern Location." Another term for Measurable might be Specific, a quality as we saw in Chapter Three, GROUNDING, that many actively avoid when it comes to finances. Nonetheless, it's necessary for us to get quite specific if we want to reach a meaningful destination.

The second component of goals is that they must also be truly AUTHENTIC, resonating with us as individuals rather than something we're choosing to please parents, partners, or peers. The same is true in our physical practice. In every single yoga class I've ever taught, while spending the majority of my time giving detailed and specific directions about the poses, I'm constantly acknowledging that these are just guidelines and that it's essential that you "move like yourself."

In fact, having taught thousands of individuals over the last two decades, I'm genuinely much more humble than when I first started. Back then I "knew" which poses were important, how to best get into them, and what the most desirable order was. Now I acknowledge that while I have increasingly large amounts of information and experience, each individual is an infinitely better authority on himself/herself than I could ever hope to be. On the physical mat, you are indeed your own best guru.

The same is true in your financial life, of course. Experts can spout statistics all day. After asking four questions in a three-minute segment, financial talk show hosts advise phone-in callers with staggering confidence. Easy, definitive answers often appeal to us because of their simplicity, but a true Warrior is always willing to battle a little longer for the truth; truth being something that usually cannot reduced to soundbites.

As an example, a few years ago, I gave a board game called CASH FLOW, which was created by RICH DAD, POOR DAD author Robert Kiyosaki, to one of my closest friends, a bestselling author, thinking we might enjoy playing it together since we were both learning more about finance. Within three minutes my friend looked through all the playing cards one draws at the beginning of the game that determine one's identity, occupation, and income, then instantly decided she could not identify with any of them. She proceeded to make her own magical identity card of "Writer/Artist/Entrepreneur." Unafraid to break the mold, my friend knew that she had to find her own unique way towards AUTHENTIC financial success and did so.

The next element to incorporate into our goal-defining process is TIME. Without assigning dates and deadlines, it's not only impossible to effectively make a plan, our desires will most probably hibernate forever as wishes. Of course, unrealistic deadlines can add to your stresses but used wisely, time can be your goal-setting friend, inspiring and guiding you throughout your journey.

Finally, and fittingly for yoga, goals must be in a category I like to call STRETCH—enough of a challenge that pursuing them is interesting and engaging but not so farfetched as to be unattainable. In the same way, when I share yoga poses I'm keenly aware of what a student's current strengths and limitations are, while at the same time intuiting what might be possible for him or her and what is not. For example, one of the physically tightest people I've ever shared yoga with was a former NFL linebacker who now hosts a Fox TV show. While a simple seated twist was perfect for his lower back issues, asking him to attempt a full split would have been sending his hamstrings on a kamikaze mission.

In a similar way, I once consulted with a client who had no problem being specific and setting a deadline but whose goals did not reflect any grounding in the present. He wanted to go from just making ends meet while swimming in credit card debt to being worth $100 million in two years. Yes, this goal was Measurable and it had a Time component and vast wealth was indeed genuinely Authentically inspiring to him—but it was completely outside the realm of the fourth component of *THE YOGA OF MONEY* Goal Setting, Stretch.

However exciting and inspiring that ostensible goal might be—unless he won the MegaMillions jackpot (chances of winning 1 in 258,890,850)—the gap between this client's present reality (struggling to meet the rent as he launched his speaking career) and its achievement was so vast it could only lead to failure and discouragement. Moreover, this goal might also have its roots in the last remaining traces of guilt over his present situation. Flamboyant ambition was over-compensating for feelings that hadn't yet been fully transformed. Self-Acceptance had not truly been achieved.

All components of MATS are necessary for a goal to be both inspiring and appropriate. Missing any element means we're engaged in fantasy, or at the other end of the spectrum, simply maintaining the status quo, rather than moving through the process of making our deepest desires real.

STEP 3: DESTINATION

Throughout this chapter, we've reconnected with our dreams and fully armed ourselves with knowledge of good goal-setting.

Each subsequent chapter in *THE YOGA OF* MONEY covers a specific financial topic, in order to enable you to craft your original goals, your personal Destinations. Throughout, please make sure evolving goals meet our MATS criterion of Measurability, Authenticity, Time, and Stretch.

Finally, it's important to remember that the Warrior does not fight alone like a vigilante. He or she is always connected with a community, able to draw on the strength of comrades, and uses every weapon available.

In our financial lives, even as we make concrete goals from each of our personal, authentic dreams, it's wise that we consult with outside experts as well, whether they be accountants or investment advisors or what we learn through extensive research. There's no need to fight our battles alone.

Through previous chapters we've grounded ourselves, left our shame behind, and now understand the aspects of goal setting. We're now ready to really dive into creating the Financial Future of your Dream Destination. It's time to plan your Victory battle by battle, beginning first with designing your Safety Net.

INVITATIONS TO PRACTICE: MIND, BODY, and BANK ACCOUNT

Mind

What does Focus feel like to you? When are you most Focused? What people/events/ things tend to disrupt your Focus and how do you best return to your true self?

Spend some time recalling your greatest Focus successes, identifying the common elements (being part of a team; being passionate about the cause). Allow yourself to enjoy remembering when and how Focus worked best for you in the past.

See how you might apply any lessons or themes to support greater Focus in your financial life now.

Body

Practice Warrior Poses along with any other standing poses (Triangle, Extended Angle) where you connect with your sense of Focus. Feel the strength of the standing poses along with the opening across the heart they require. Let the steady gaze remind you of the power of your own ability to Focus.

As you stand firm in each shape, explore how you are embodying a Spiritual Warrior with an open and compassionate heart.

Bank Account

Here's a recap of the Goal Setting steps I shared for you to apply to any aspect of your financial or personal life:

1. Dreaming & Remembering. Really give yourself the time to uncover your past passions and discover any brave new dreams that are almost ready to emerge.

2. Explore Defining your goals, including the elements of **MATS**:

Measurable

Authentic

Time-Bound

Stretch

3. Destination: as we explore more aspects of your personal financial life in subsequent chapters, keep applying steps 1 and 2 to create for yourself a path towards the financial Destination of your Dreams.

CHAPTER 5

BALANCING

TREE POSE

"Man plans. God laughs"
~ Yiddish Proverb

BALANCE POSES •
CENTERING & CREATING A SAFETY NET

Tree Pose is perhaps the most classic balance pose: the one someone in a yogurt commercial performs to signal, "I'm doing yoga."

It seems deceptively simple: standing on one leg, you bend your other knee and slide the foot up the inner thigh, attempting to balance. Hands may be held at the heart in prayer or more dramatically lifted to the sky like tree limbs. The pose might be easily accomplished by a beginner, and yet paradoxically an advanced student might find it challenging on a day when his or her balance is off. (And yes, that happens; as in life, one's yoga balancing skills vary from day to day.)

Calling this shape Tree Pose accurately reflects the true nature of BALANCE. Balance means not being frozen and immobile like a statue. If a tree is too rigid, it will easily break during the first strong wind. If it is too flexible, though, it will bend too far and be uprooted. A balance between being grounded and firm and yet negotiating the stormy challenges of life is required for a tree—or a person—to thrive.

The same is true for our Financial Practice. We need to be centered and grounded as we establish and work toward our goals, but we also need to be flexible enough to realize that nothing ever goes exactly according to plan.

That's why having a Safety Net (a phrase I vastly prefer to the more dramatic "Emergency Fund") makes such good sense. Indeed, establishing a fund is almost always the first step in getting one's financial house in order.

While yoga is inherently optimistic and life-enhancing, we never deny that certain situations are beyond our immediate control. Unforeseen circumstances like corporate downsizing or an unexpected illness will affect our lives and our finances. *MONEY* magazine reports that 78% of us will have a major negative event within 10 years, so it seems basic common sense to have some kind of plan in place as part of our Practice.

We'll begin our discussion by referencing traditional benchmarks. There's a lot of variety in these general rules, however. Most financial experts suggest having three to six months of income in reserve. Dave Ramsey says starting with $1,000 and building up gradually is fine, while Suze Orman believes one really needs eight months of income saved as soon as possible. Obviously, there's a huge difference between $1,000 and eight months of income. How do you determine how much is really necessary for you? Eschewing cookie-cutter formulas, *THE YOGA OF MONEY* takes you through Six Steps to craft your own most appropriate Safety Net.

STEP ONE: First, we'll look more carefully at our numbers. In Chapter Three, GROUNDING, we got a handle on our current spending, calculating our monthly "Nut." Now, since we want to be as grounded and flexible as Tree Pose, it's time to examine this in greater detail.

In the yoga sutras (the most ancient Sanskrit texts) Tree Pose—indeed, each and every yoga poses—must have two qualities: *sthira* (strong/hard/fixed) and *sukham* (easy/soft/fluid). In finance, parallel traditional terms would be "non-discretionary" or fixed cost items such as mortgages, auto loans, and insurance premiums and "discretionary," those where there is more "wiggle room" such as restaurants, entertainment, and gifts. Thus, Step One of our Safety Net construction process is to determine which of our expenses are Fixed (*sthira*) and which are Fluid (*sukham*).

This ratio may vary enormously from individual to individual. We may learn that although our monthly nut is $5,000 based on current spending, only $2,000 of that falls into the Fixed category while $3,000 is Fluid. The opposite might also be true, where we learn that very little of our spending is discretionary. What matters is that we take this closer look at how cash actually flows through our lives.

STEP TWO examines the Fixed category in greater detail since often things are not quite as fixed as we think. My landlord might be intractable about the amount and the due date of my rent, but I once had a car loan that allowed me to skip a payment every six months if the account was current. Another credit card of mine currently offers a payment protection plan where minimums would be met in the case of unemployment or hardship. It is absolutely worth researching one's options when it comes to "fixed" items ranging from student loan forbearance to unemployment eligibility and benefits.

STEP THREE for setting up your Safety Net is to sit with the Fluid items and see how discretionary they really are. Would giving up your weekly massage (or downgrading your cable package) be a minor inconvenience or would it actually have deeper consequences to your sense of wellbeing? Of course extravagant nights on the town might need to be cut back when facing unemployment, even if there's no explicit networking potential, the camaraderie of good friends might be essential during one's economic downturn. What your accountant might dismiss as frivolity might be for you an absolute essential (and vice versa as we'll see in Step Five). As with all things in our Practice, approaching this self-discovery with honesty and without judgment is vital.

Having a new, deeper understanding of our own Fixed and Fluid numbers, STEP FOUR now asks us to look outside ourselves and towards the marketplace in general. A highly specialized college professor subject to a complex hiring process via various committees faces very different challenges than the NYC waiter willing to take any gig to meet the rent between acting auditions.

It's important that we fine-tune an awareness of how challenging a setback might be for you. The untenured professor might need to budget six months to a year to find a comparable position, whereas the waiter might call everyone in his/her acting class and be able to obtain a catering job for the next day. Of course, no one can see the future, but we must assess our situation based on the past and the present realities of our field of employment.

Having grounded ourselves in the world of our own Numbers and the economic climate around them, *THE YOGA OF MONEY* now returns us to the world of Mindset in STEP FIVE.

It's time to gain a clearer understanding of our comfort with uncertainty and risk tolerance. We have to look inward at ourselves. Beyond asking obvious questions such as "For whom besides yourself are you responsible financially...?", it's time to contemplate, for example, "How attached are you to your current living situation?" Are taking in a roommate, subletting your two-bedroom in favor of a temporary tiny sublet, or even moving cross-country for a new job opportunity really viable options, or is your top priority maintaining the current housing status quo? Again, there are no right or wrong answers here, but it's vital to have a clear and honest sense of your ability to flow with change.

During our exploration of STEP FIVE, it's important to note that our risk tolerance may have almost nothing to do with our Number Reality and entirely to do with our temperament. For example, I once consulted with a major magazine editor about possible new directions in her creative life, and it quickly became clear that her switching to a freelance lifestyle looked perfectly fine on paper—she had a nine month severance package—but was untenable for her utterly risk-averse temperament. As another example of risk-aversion extremes, I currently have a 26-year-old friend who will borrow cab fare home to Williamsburg, confident she'll pay me back and make the rest of her overdue rent in tips at her coat check job at a dive bar over the weekend (but only if it rains), and another 32-year-old who has confided that he cannot sleep at night when his emergency fund dips below $2 million. Clearly, there is no universal magic formula whereby "X Dollars in the Bank = Peace of Mind."

Only after having gone through both the Numbers and the Mindset exercises are we now ready for STEP SIX: Self-Determining our Safety Net. We may have started with the conventional three to six month wisdom, but we can now re-assess what amount suits us best based on our five previous self-evaluations.

ONE JOURNEY ON CREATING A SAFETY NET

As an illustration of how and why each individual's Safety Net must be holistically crafted (versus relying on boilerplate formulas), I worked through these steps with my 26-year-old coat check friend, Rosie in the first YOGA OF MONEY Mastermind Group.

Having gone through the GROUNDING exercises in Chapter 3, Rosie learned that her monthly nut was approximately $3,140.

In STEP ONE, when she looked closely at those numbers she saw that $1,840 of that was Fixed. The largest expenses were $995 in rent for her shared Williamsburg sublet; $280 towards her $25,000 of student loans; and four or more daily $2.75 subway rides that cost over $200 a month.*

Her Fluid category was just that—extremely fluid—and varied quite a bit each month. On average, she tends to spend approximately $800 on food and drink and, since she aspires to a career as a red carpet fashion stylist, even while buying vintage and often making her own outfits, she still spends at least $800 a month on clothes and accessories.

Going through STEP TWO—examining her Fixed Categories more carefully—Rosie discovered that, in an emergency situation such as unemployment, she could in fact suspend her credit card payments for up to six months ($50 less a month) and also postpone her student loan payments for up to a

---

* While no longer supported by her parents, they had agreed to cover her health insurance under their small business owner's policy.

year (although they would still accumulate interest). Thus, during a personal downturn, she could (temporarily) spend $330 less a month than during flush times.

Examining these Fixed Costs also had two other interesting side effects. First, Rosie realized that for $116.50 she could buy a subway pass for an entire month, something she'd been reluctant to do since paying over $100 didn't feel comfortable all at once. After she understood that she'd be saving $50 to $80 a month, though, this became a more attractive and obvious money saver. Second, Rosie realized that she and her roommates practically never watch HBO together as they'd originally thought they would. Wi-Fi and a Hulu/Netflix combination would save them each $35 per month. These two easy modifications—with no sacrifice on her part—saved her over $100 a month.

With just these two minor economic adjustments and knowing that if suddenly unemployed she could suspend two fixed payments in a Safety Net Situation, her Fixed Costs in a temporary crisis could drop from $1,840 to $1,300 a month. In other words, if she had to, she could pay more than $540 less—a nearly 30% reduction in expenses—during a lean period.

STEP THREE—examining one's Fluid Category—with Rosie was an entirely different kind of adventure. While she realized that a weekly shop at Trader Joe's would drastically reduce her eating out costs, her entire reason to be in New York was to be out and about at night, to be "seen on the scene" by fellow fashionistas, gaining Instagram followers while making the widest array of social and business connections possible. "I didn't move to New York City to stay in at night and watch the same basic cable shows I could in Phoenix," she declared. Even more striking was her commitment to her fashion budget. Rosie would frankly rather have lost a limb than reduce her ever-expanding wardrobe. Ultimately (and somewhat ironically), for Rosie Fluid Costs were far more fixed than Fixed Costs!

STEP FOUR—looking at the bigger picture of her industry and the larger economic factors around how she earned money—revealed that while this particular coat check job paid well enough in tips, with all of Rosie's connections and particularly via her Instagram followers, finding a similar substitute would be relatively easy. In fact, during the summer months she'd often accept other part-time gigs to bolster her income while sketching her own designs. With her vast social network and her great flexibility/indifference to how she earned money before hitting it big as a stylist, finding another source of equivalent income did not seem daunting.

STEP FIVE—an assessment of her Mindset around risk-taking—held little surprise when it revealed that Rosie was quite comfortable with uncertainty. Truly, the only thing that mattered to her was getting closer to the center of the city's nightlife and immersing herself in the world of fashion. Even a "worst case scenario" of unexpected unemployment resulting in a season of couch surfing did not frighten her in the least (as long as there was Wi-Fi and a decent subway line nearby).

For Rosie, building a traditional six month cash reserve felt so overwhelming that she wasn't even willing to start. Yet, as she completed STEP SIX—synthesizing all of the above inquiries—Rosie realized that while she was relatively comfortable living on the edge—always having enough or just nearly enough to get through a month—that the amount actually required for her to feel an entirely new level of security was surprisingly modest. If she had as little as $3,000 saved—or even $2,000 since her month-to-month sublet meant very little to her—Rosie knew she could get through any of life's unexpected speed bumps without any major disruption or stress. Simply pocketing away $40 of tips from each of her four weekly shifts at the clubs meant that within a month or two she could construct a Safety Net that would allow her to be her utterly fabulous self with a vastly increased sense of financial confidence.

While Rosie concluded that contrary to the standard advice of having at least six months of savings in an emergency fund, even a "One Month's Income Safety Net" was enough to quintuple her sense of security, my multi-millionaire buddy going through this same process came to his own very different realizations.

Joshua has two kids to support and a $15,000 a month mortgage on his Tribeca loft. He works at a hedge fund and, although his salary would seem stratospheric to most people, he works in an industry vastly more susceptible to the swings of the stock market than Rosie's dive bar employment. More importantly, his financial temperament is completely different from Rosie's.

Joshua and I went through these same steps informally over a pricy bottle of Cabernet, and we managed to loosen his attachment to a relatively arbitrary dollar figure of $2 million in an Emergency Account. Instead, he realized that for him, having two years of expenses saved (covering his mortgage, private school tuitions, and a slight reduction in his luxury lifestyle) is more than sufficient for him to feel financial peace. Even if the market crashed or his firm went under, he trusted that within a year or two he'd be back to his former earnings.

Existing at different extremes of the spectrum, boilerplate advice simply did not work for either one of my friends. Uncovering and crafting their own best Safety Nets did. That's why the *YOGA OF MONEY* offers an individual, non-cookie cutter approach that allows each of us to personally decide what's necessary to satisfy our need for security and our unique tree-like balance of groundedness and flexibility.

Just by completing the exercises and knowing our Safety Net goal, we can get closer to peace of mind. This is because while our natural knee-jerk reaction to crisis tends to be rushing into Problem Solving Mode, this specific inquiry keeps us grounded in the Spirit of Practice. What if instead of experiencing panic, we were bolstered by our Safety Net and able to re-label those challenging situations as opportunities to deepen our Practice? Might it be possible to view whatever unexpected crisis we're facing as our friend, or better yet, our teacher?

Of course, such balancing lessons are infinitely easier to appreciate in retrospect. All of us have painful experiences (a divorce, getting fired) that we retroactively describe as being "ironically, the best thing that ever happened to me." I certainly do. What if, however, we attempted to bridge the gap of time between that ultimate realization and this current moment by not rushing in trying to fix everything all at once? What if our Practice Mode (bolstered by our now clarified and self-defined Safety Nets) allowed us to learn from the actual experience rather than running away from it?

Ultimately, redefining our setbacks and emergencies as balancing challenges that strengthen us far more than a state of perpetual ease and stability, reaches to the heart of *THE YOGA OF MONEY.*

Beyond knowing that "a smooth sea never made a strong sailor", our process of inquiry here also teaches us invaluable lessons about who we are and what we value, fully engaging us in the holistic spirit of Practice.

INVITATIONS TO PRACTICE: MIND, BODY, and BANK ACCOUNT

Mind

Explore and define what balance means to you in all aspects of your life. When are you most balanced? When are you least? What are the ways you've learned to come back to a state of ease and equilibrium? Can you expand and develop those practices, or simply practice them more often?

A balanced life, like a balanced bank account, incorporates both positive and negative aspects, joys and disappointments. Examine if you are allowing yourself the full richness of whatever experience life offers you.

Body

Practice Tree Pose, along with any other balancing poses such as Warrior III, Shiva Nataraja, and even Side Plank.

As you explore the self-imposed challenge of balancing on one limb rather than two, allow yourself to really feel the qualities of *sthira* and *sukham* in your body.

Notice what feelings come up when your balance gets shaky and what kind of Focus helps bring you back most effectively.

Bank
Account

Following the guidelines in this chapter, apply the concept of balance to set-up (or refine) your Safety Net. To summarize the steps again:

1. Determine which expenses are fixed and which are fluid.
2. Look more carefully at the fixed expenses.
3. Do the same for the fluid category.
4. Examine the practical realities of your world and how you earn money.

5. Honestly assess your personal tolerance towards risk.

6. Based on all these inquiries, Self-Determine what's best Safety Net for you.

CHAPTER 6

TRANSFORMATION

HEADSTAND

"Be realistic—plan for a miracle."

~ Osho

GOING UPSIDE DOWN •
GOING INTO DEBT

Inversions are poses where we completely shift our perspective. In headstand, handstand, and forearm-stand, in defiance of gravity (and sometimes common sense), we quite literally go upside down, giving us a dramatic moment of TRANSFORMATION.

Headstand is usually achieved by having the student kneeling a few inches from the wall. There are multiple variations, but usually the first step is to place the top of the head on the ground and interlace the fingers at the back of the neck. With bent legs, one walks the feet closer to the face until there's no more room, and a tiny hop upward launches them vertically. Ultimately, this becomes smooth and effortless, but especially in the beginning proper alignment and a short stay in the shape are required to prevent injury.

Inversions are particularly seductive poses for many reasons. They have tremendous physical benefits for the body, often resulting in a rush of energy and mood elevation. In fact, inversions are often nicknamed the "Ecstasy Poses" because of their euphoric aftereffects. There are several ancient yoga texts that speak of their "youthenizing" powers as well as numerous modern studies that document the physiological benefits of going upside down. In short, inversions are both good for you and they make you feel great.

In our financial lives, often a similar kind of rush happens when we get into debt. We desire something—whether it's as practical as a car, a home, an education, or as non-essential but enjoyable as a new pair of Manolos or a week in the Bahamas—that we cannot afford. Paying on credit can immediately deliver the thrill of Christmas morning to us, but ultimately there's a price that must be paid. That's why Inversions and Debt both have the power to utterly Transform our bodies and our lives, but at the same time there are risks we must address.

In our Physical Practice, there are such tremendous benefits to going upside down that Headstand is often nicknamed "The King of the Poses." At the same time, the neck was obviously not designed to support the weight of the entire body for extended periods of time. When teaching a student how to do a headstand, I increase their time in the pose by five, at the most ten, seconds per week. The paradox is that being upside down temporarily yields health benefits and even a sense of ecstasy, but at the same time being upside too long can cause serious physical damage. Yes, we can enjoy our awesome adventure, but we should make sure the roller coaster's safety bar is securely fastened.

The reality is that debt is a part of almost everyone's financial universe. In fact, approximately 80% of Americans currently have some form of debt. If we exclude secured debt (things we generally term "good," like homes and cars), we are still left with 50% of the population owing money to someone, somewhere, most often on credit cards. And those numbers are truly staggering.

Credit card debt surged to $57.1 billon last year, with more than half of the population defining themselves as "financially insecure." Right now, the average American household credit card debt hovers at $15,609, a large contributing factor to the more than a million Americans filing for bankruptcy annually.

Even for those who more or less make ends meet, going into debt is often a secret shame that most people sweep under the rug. In fact, more than 35% of the population has an average debt of $5,178 that is so overdue it has been reported to collection agencies. Think about that: for every three people you pass in the street in New York City, one of them is likely to be receiving calls and letters from a debt collector demanding payment.

All of this demonstrates why managing debt properly is a cornerstone of modern financial health, one we cannot overlook in *THE YOGA OF MONEY.* Healthy debt can create a home for our family or provide us with an education that enriches our lives and our income.

On the other hand, when car and home loans become greater than the value of the asset (i.e., you owe more money on an item than it is actually worth), they are referred to as "upside down." Like a headstand sustained for too long, this is an unstable, even damaging financial situation.

Bankruptcy would, of course, represent the final conclusion of a financial journey that's gone irretrievably south. Sometimes bankruptcy is truly the best course of action, allowing for a fresh start and new beginnings but more often than not, there are ways of turning our financial lives "right-side up."

ONE JOURNEY ON TRANSFORMING DEBT

Claudia and I have been friends since college and for three years in the early 90s we shared a loft on the Lower East Side, both of us working the graveyard shift doing graphic presentations for an investment bank worth 1.062 trillion dollars.

During this time she completed her PhD in English from Columbia and I finished an indie film and became a yoga instructor. Throughout the period, we lent each other rent money back and forth more times than I care to count.

Claudia has also participated in every *YOGA OF MONEY* workshop, online course, and Mastermind to date. In short, we've spent over two decades sharing our Money Journey together.

Claudia's financially comfortable, academically-minded parents were willing to finance her graduate school expenses, allowing her to emerge with, in her own words, "a highly marketable expertise in Ancient Greek Philosophy," but they provided nothing beyond tuition, books, and a laptop upgrade. Thus, during eight years of graduate school, Claudia worked part-time doing presentations for billionaires while accumulating over $28,000 in credit card debt.

As she sought her first teaching position in a highly competitive and specialized job market, within a year that figure soared to $48,000. Only after she'd maxed out every card and was then declined for two new accounts did she decide to stop waiting for a MacArthur Genius Grant to solve all her financial problems.

Initially feeling overwhelmed by the entire situation, Claudia went to several Debtor's Anonymous meetings but "failed" all their tests to see if she had an addiction. She wasn't a compulsive debtor. She'd just gotten herself into a bad situation. She did, however, learn some basic guidelines from those Debtor's Anonymous meetings, including a steadfast resolution to accumulate no further debt. She also learned that she was not alone, that blaming herself wasn't particularly productive, and perhaps most importantly, that others in even worse situations had found a way out.

A brilliant student and researcher, Claudia then quickly mastered getting-out-of-debt basics. Having spent nearly a decade making "pretty flow charts and lovely pie graphs" for billion dollar mergers, she found it ironic that she'd never taken a square look at her own numbers on a spreadsheet. For the first time ever, fully embodying the concept of GROUNDING, Claudia created an Excel document for her own finances in order to construct a debt repayment plan. She created columns for each credit card, the annual APR, the minimum payment required, and its due date.

Armed with this information, for three months she tried the SNOWBALL METHOD, prioritizing paying off her credit cards in order of highest interest rate. While this made sense on her spreadsheet, it was somehow less than satisfying in real life. Progress was definitely being made, but it still felt as though she were fighting an endless, uphill battle.

Claudia did a little more research on debt repayment and switched to the LADDER METHOD: paying off the smallest debts first so they disappear from the spreadsheet entirely. That's when something inside her shifted. Although it made more sense on a balance sheet to pay an extra $100 towards her $7,500 Capital One Card balance (24% APR) than the $400 balance on her Nordstrom's Card (11.9% APR), it was much more emotionally satisfying to work towards bringing the latter card down to a zero balance.

At the same time, Claudia also found she liked the challenge of transferring balances to lower interest cards. Moving balances around didn't decrease them, but once she fully understood the math, the advantages were astonishing.

For example, paying $1000 a month towards her $48,000 debt at 24% APR would take 163 months (more than thirteen years) to complete and meant accumulating $114,000 interest on that original $48,000, while paying the exact same amount at 12% APR meant the interest would come to $17,000 and would take about 66 months (five and a half years).

Excited by the challenge of it all, Claudia switched balances to several cards that promoted 0% APR for introductory periods (several months to over a year), moving the debt again whenever it was wise to do so.

Finally, Claudia tapped into her humanities background, discovering that perhaps the most powerful part of her debt repayment process was creating a visual representation of it that highlighted her progress. Traipsing to the art store with a painter boyfriend, she charged a 30" x 40" canvas for $91.38, and then ceremoniously cut up her very last credit card. On the canvas she doodled 480 oval swirls with a black sharpie, each one representing $100 of the money she owed.

For every $100 she paid, Claudia colored one in with bright, bold colors, creating a vivid and expansive tableau of her progress. She hung the canvas in her bedroom, encouraged each time she saw the blossoming image expanding.

Although the painter boyfriend was gone after two years, the winning combination of 1) no more credit card spending, 2) transferring balances whenever possible, 3) the enthusiasm of paying off individual accounts, and 4) the sheer fun of seeing her momentum in bright colors on her wall allowed her to be debt free in just under four years.

When I asked Claudia recently if she regretted the experience of getting into such major debt, she paused to reflect before answering, "At first, 'Yes.' There were moments of tremendous anxiety where I felt that I'd painted myself into a corner and that somehow at 32, I'd made foolish choices that could cost me hundreds of thousands dollars and even haunt me for the rest of my life. But once I figured out that the situation was indeed quite solvable—and that I could even have some fun with the process—I changed my mind about it all. Maybe I did make some classically foolish choices in my late 20s by spending money I didn't have, but now I no longer regret them. Whether it was the lavish Valentine's gift for a boyfriend I broke up with two weeks later, or the week in the Bahamas I treated myself to after I successfully defended my dissertation, I don't feel guilty about those experiences. I don't even think of them as mistakes, though knowing what I know now about interest rates, I won't ever repeat those kinds of adventures with my credit cards again. And to be totally honest, I'm actually glad that this became a kind of Wake Up Call towards becoming conscious of how I spend money and an invitation to get the rest of my financial house in order before I hit 40. I went from being clueless and overwhelmed to being self-reliant and financially savvy."

"Milking my dissertation for what it's worth," Claudia concluded, "Marcus Aurelius wasn't writing about my experiences transferring balances in 150 AD but this perfectly sums up how I transformed my financial situation and emerged debt free: "The first rule is to keep an untroubled spirit. The second is to look things in the face and know them for what they are."

It's interesting that even in straightforward business-speak that "Forgiveness" is the term used to describe the dissolution of debt. Just as we let go of negative feelings and injuries to forgive another person who has wronged us, in the same way we have to release negative emotions around debt, the circumstances and choices that got us into those situations, and perhaps most importantly, our unkind feelings towards ourselves. Forgiveness is really an amplification of Self–Acceptance, the first and most vital step in our Practice before any Transformation can occur.

Ultimately, the ebb and flow of finances is as natural as our own breathing. Unless we can pay for our homes in cash or have saved enough for our children's schooling, invariably, there will be moments on our balance sheet when there's more red ink than we'd like to see. Our awareness of this—and our Acceptance—will allow us to find a healthy, judgment-free approach to our debt.

Indeed, as the Sufi poet Hafiz said nearly 700 years ago:

"Even after all this time, the sun never
says to the earth 'you owe me.'
Look what happens with a love like
that. It lights the whole sky."

~ Hafiz

INVITATIONS TO PRACTICE: MIND, BODY, and BANK ACCOUNT

Mind

Since by definition debt is always about the past, here's where we might find that our greatest challenge is embracing Forgiveness. What memories of our past would be wisest to release, not forgetting necessarily but truly forgiving?

Perhaps even more than individuals or events, we might realize we need to find ways to forgive ourselves for any decisions we may regret. We are often our own harshest critics, judging ourselves with far less mercy than we would show towards anyone else.

Fully explore all the ways you can cultivate the spirit of Forgiveness towards your financial past and then apply them with compassion and enthusiasm.

Body

While I encourage you to practice the more dramatic Inversions such as headstand, handstand, and forearm stand under the guidance of a good teacher, more easily obtainable forms of going upside down also have tremendous benefits. Remember that Inversions include any pose where the head is below the heart. A pose that's accessible as Downward Dog, for example, also reverses your perspective and gives your spine a chance to lengthen.

Keep in mind that Inversions (like Debt) must be approached mindfully, particularly given the rush of excitement they offer.

Bank Account

Allow yourself to come face-to-face with all your debts.

For some, this can be an utterly overwhelming step.

Again, it's not necessary to approach this as a dramatic wake-up call where you rip the band-aid off, bracing yourself for the sting.

Instead, approach this step with compassion and forgiveness, knowing that being Grounded about our numbers is a major step in welcoming Transformation, but only if it is accompanied by Self-Acceptance.

Before you leap into action to use the strategies in the next chapter about Backward Planning to devise your best repayment strategy, make sure you've come to a place of Reconnection via all the poses and practices you've been learning.

CHAPTER 7

CHALLENGE

FLYING CROW

"It's kind of fun to do the impossible."

~ Walt Disney

ARM BALANCES •
ACHIEVING "IMPOSSIBLE" GOALS

No matter the level of one's athleticism, part of the allure of a yoga practice is that there's a perpetual element of CHALLENGE. There's always a new variation on a pose or an innovative new way to explore opening the body. Not only is our curiosity and sense of adventure continually stimulated, there's also the thrilling moment where what was once impossible becomes possible. Nothing represents this more vividly than arm balances, poses where, with only the hands on the ground, the body floats in mid-air.

Flying Crow is one such pose, and a particularly spectacular and challenging one at that. Hands on the ground, leaning forward, the elbows form a shelf as a bent shin is placed across it. Everything but the hands lifts up in the air, the entire body floating seemingly effortlessly in defiance of gravity (and, again, common sense, since we can and often do fall flat on our faces as we learn to balance)!

Arm balances almost never "just happen" on the first try. Unlike a simple, wake-up stretch from a nap, they are not inherently "natural." I've never demonstrated Flying Crow and had a student respond, "Oh yeah. I do that all the time." Instead, almost every student requires extensive instruction followed by plenty of practice.

Poses like Flying Crow are full of multiple kinds of challenges, both physical and psychological. First, one accrues patience and flexibility while opening up the hips over time. Next, one develops resolve by strengthening the arms, shoulders, and the core. Finally, having mastered the physical challenges, one deepens one's courage by leaning the body forward enough to risk falling. Often this combination of challenges can seem daunting.

In the same way, in our financial lives there are long term goals—such as buying a home—which may at first seem far off fantasies that are completely out of reach. For example, CNBC reports that the <u>average</u> apartment price in Manhattan reached a staggering $1.72 million in 2014. Beyond real estate, other items in this category might include further education or college for one's children. The average state school now costs $9,000 a year while Ivy League tuition and fees are just under $50,000 annually. This means that the the cost of educating a baby born today at a state school will amount to roughly $150,000. Confronted with such constantly inflating numbers, it's easy to become discouraged.

Applying some yogic principles of Practice, however, can transform what initially seems impossible into something very real. The most ancient of the yoga texts, the sutras from approximately 400 CE, say that a successful practice must have three qualities: Time, Consistency, and Enthusiasm. The same is true for our Challenge Goals in the world of money.

First, let's explore the aspect of Time. The physical benefits of yoga are extremely potent but rarely instantaneous. As Dr. Timothy McCall writes, "Yoga is strong medicine but slow medicine." I've seen people heal themselves and transform their bodies through yoga, but it rarely happens overnight. When a new and eager 42-year-old student who works as an investment banker asks me how long before she gets flexible, I always respond by asking her how long it took to get tight.

This quality of patience also applies to our financial lives. Get Rich Quick schemes invariably fail. It simply takes time for legitimate investments to mature. Releasing my runner's hamstrings into a full split took three years of almost daily work. Analogously, stocks double on average every 7.5 years. In other words, yes, major opening can be achieved in a one hour yoga session, but massive transformation of the body simply takes time, just as achieving our major financial goals do.

In addition to an awareness of Time, it is not enough that you practice yoga over a long period; you must also do so with Consistency. We have to keep showing up frequently on a steady basis. Simply taking an occasional yoga class each month over several decades is definitely not going to produce powerful physical changes.

Of course our financial lives require the same consistency as our yoga practice. We have to establish a way of budgeting and developing regular savings habits that makes sense for our personalities and our goals. Even if we stash away a modest sum and forty years later discover that it's multiplied into a small fortune, we cannot simply "check out" of the ins and outs of our day-to-day finances during those decades.

Finally, it is not just enough to have Consistency over Time. According to the yoga sutras, we must practice with sincere Enthusiasm, a key component of which we've mentioned via our MATS criterion of Authenticity. Your Practice, whether yogic or financial, must have goals that are really yours and yours alone. Whether it's getting your foot behind your head or buying a vacation home, the goal has to be meaningful and inspiring for you.

Now we're ready to roll up our sleeves and address the Numbers components of our journey via Backwards Planning.

CREATING A BACKWARDS PLAN

After defining our desired end result (Home Ownership or an Education, for example), we then plan each step backwards until we reach the present. If we want our toddler to attend Yale, we project how much that's going to cost and then create a plan that carries us through the next 16 years so that can happen.

This technique can be used for any project or goal, of course. I've worked with writers with seemingly overwhelming due dates, working backwards from

Ultimate Steps like "Hand in Final Manuscript to Publisher," preceded by "Incorporate Proofreader's Final Changes," all the way through to Steps One and Two, "Re-read Notes for Incomplete Chapters" and "Write Ad for Research Assistant."

Although on a physical and a financial level, our "Impossible" goals can seem very daunting at first, the element of challenge in a pose or our financial life is, of course, a great blessing of our Practice. It keeps us showing up and offers us numerous incremental rewards along each step of the path. Ultimately, floating one day in a seemingly impossible arm balance like Flying Crow—or walking through the door of your very own home—serves as a powerful reminder that when we apply Time, Consistency, and Enthusiasm (and a solid Backwards Plan and Budgeting System), truly anything is possible.

INVITATIONS TO PRACTICE: MIND, BODY, and BANK ACCOUNT

Mind

Recall your own previously "impossible" achievements. For example, for all of us there was a time before we knew how to walk. Somehow, despite countless falls, every physically-able human does learn to stand up on two feet.

The same is true for your financial and life challenges. Invariably, someone else has achieved what you are setting out to do, whether that's buying a home, attending college, or starting your own business. Rather than indulging in a series of arguments against yourself about how others somehow had greater advantages, reframe the argument in your favor. If they can do it, so can you. Positive thinking alone cannot win the battle, but it is nonetheless a vital component of any long-term success strategy.

Body

Arm Balances like Flying Crow are excellent metaphors and practices to explore the concept of Challenge and Long-Term Goals.

For many though, impressive arm balances can feel too far out of reach. For others, they might be quite accessible where another seemingly easier pose might feel unattainable. What's important is that your Challenge Pose be in the realm of Stretch for you (remember our MATS criterion). The particular experience of Stretch will vary considerably from individual to individual.

For many, a classic hip opener like ankle-to-knee pose will offer a rich opportunity to be present with lively sensations of opening over a long period of time. For others, *Hanuman*—a full split named for the mountain-straddling Monkey God— might offer a journey that takes months or years.

In fact, the full expression of a pose might forever elude you, but the lessons offered are available from the very first attempt. You may never have a photograph of yourself in a difficult pose on your Christmas card, but that doesn't mean it hasn't benefited you on every level.

Explore the concept of backwards planning for each of your current and evolving financial goals. Start at the final destination and work methodically backward, step by step.

Bank Account

The most future-oriented steps might currently be general, but definitely stick with the exercise until you have some immediate and near-future steps that feel concrete and do-able.

If a feeling of overwhelm arises—"I'll never get there!"—renew all the re-connecting and centering practices we've explored before.

Remember that by definition as your Stretch/Challenge, your goal has to be currently out of reach. Beyond the practical task of mapping out a road map so that it can become a reality, what you're really doing is paving the way for a journey that's one not only of expansion, but that's also joyful throughout.

CHAPTER 8

FLEXIBILITY

WHEEL POSE

"Playing it safe is very risky."

~ Seth Godin

BACKBENDING & INVESTMENT •
RISKS AND REWARDS

As we age, there's a cultural expectation that we grow brittle and closed off, that our spines stiffen, and our range of motion decreases dramatically over the years. Indeed, often the number-one reason that initially draws people to a yoga class is the desire for increased FLEXIBILITY and the fear of losing this as they age.

Having warmed the body up sufficiently, we begin our more serious backbending towards the end of class. Perhaps chief amongst backbends is Wheel Pose. Lying on one's back, knees bent and feet on the ground, with hands framing the ears, one straightens the arms and legs, lifting the chest to the sky. And, of course, there are much more easily attainable version of Wheel Pose such as Supported Half Wheel that almost anyone can do with the aid of a simple yoga block underneath the sacrum.

Backbends are also known as "heart-openers" because just like a puppy asking us to scratch its belly, we leave ourselves open and exposed. Energetically, they are about expansion, and expansion inherently involves risk taking. That's why, often more than physical limitations such as lack of arm strength or tight shoulders, the most common barrier to this and other backbending poses is Fear.

In the financial world, investment always involves a degree of risk and uncertainty. As with Wheel Pose, we have to be prepared and really ready—warmed-up as it were—before we start exploring investment as a way to increase our net worth. This means that not only should we be fully informed and knowledgeable about all aspects of risk, we must also be in a secure enough position where we're investing money we can afford to lose.

That's why, whenever I teach backbending, I'm aware that while fear may be the greatest obstacle, it is neither illegitimate nor something to ignore. Both the super-stiff and the super-bendy are prone to injuries if they're not self-aware in their practice. In the same way, the naive investor, along with overly aggressive or cautious ones, might be setting themselves up for poor returns and even significant losses.

Just as I would never push a student beyond his or her current level of flexibility, in the same way we must each find the right financial strategies that match our goals and our comfort level around expansion and uncertainty.

It's important to become educated about the vast array of investment possibilities, ranging from mutual funds, IRAs, stocks, T-bills, to more speculative high-risk ventures. Just as I would never want to push a student's spine beyond its current flexibility, in the same way we want our investment choices to be adventurous yet informed, and most importantly, appropriate for us. Clarifying the risks and rewards of different investment strategies—along with an understanding of both one's financial goals and temperament—allows us an experience that is both safe AND expansive.

On the yoga mat this translates to my assisting a very limber student in a full wheel from a handstand while suggesting to another less flexible person that a gentle, supported half-wheel using a yoga block as a prop would be the wisest move.

Flexibility also relates to expanding our capacities to give and extend our talents and goods. It's both karmic logic and common sense to believe that the more we give, the more we will receive. Sometimes this means leaving our comfort zone and attempting to reach a broader audience. Other times it means investing in ourselves through further education and training. And, of course, sometimes it means taking the calculated risks of branching out and offering something new and fresh to the world.

What's vital is that we listen to the messages from our heart to find the right path for us now.

Investments and backbending can provide us with tremendous increases in heart-opening and wealth, but only after we have managed to wisely assess and navigate the risks and rewards of expansion.

Being in touch with our fears and vulnerability, particularly about expansion, is vital for us to enjoy all the Abundance that's waiting for us.

INVITATIONS TO PRACTICE: MIND, BODY, and BANK ACCOUNT

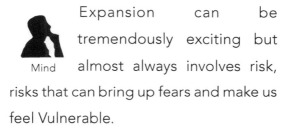 Expansion can be tremendously exciting but almost always involves risk, risks that can bring up fears and make us feel Vulnerable.

Mind

Yet one of the great paradoxes highlighted by Brené Brown in her famous TED talk is that Vulnerability can be powerful. It connects us to our hearts and our humanity.

What fears do you have around money? What might be holding you back from the truly abundant life you desire and deserve?

In your exploration, consider not only that the LACK of money might trigger deep-seated fears and other emotions, but an ABUNDANCE of money could also provoke other issues as well.

Listening to our heart's messages must take place for our entire lifetime. That's why this is such a vital skill to develop in our *YOGA OF MONEY* practice.

Body

Major Backbends like Full Wheel are dynamic and powerful ways of opening up our hearts.

Much subtler, more easily attainable versions, however, such as a supported half-wheel where one lies down and simply places a yoga block underneath the sacrum can also reestablish this connection.

Simpler still, all you need to do is sit comfortably, close your eyes, and placing a hand on your heart, ask and wait to receive any messages.

What's essential is that one simply be open to whatever arises, neither anticipating nor judging what your heart wants to communicate through your body.

 Investments can be straightforward and relatively uncomplicated (such as T-Bills) to highly complex and byzantine (like hedge funds for those with significant assets) .

Bank Account

As you explore the right pathway for yourself—perhaps with the aid of a trusted financial professional—never lose touch with the messages from your heart about the right combination of risk and security that best suits your individual journey.

CHAPTER 9

RELAXATION & SUPPORT

GODDESS POSE

"80 percent of life is showing up."

~ Woody Allen

RESTORATIVE POSES •
SETTING THINGS UP FOR RETIREMENT

After the expansive boldness of backbending, it's time to take things down several notches. We need poses that allow us to focus inward with a more quieting, calming energy. It's time for lingering forward bends, hip openers, and most importantly, restorative poses. Goddess Pose is many people's favorite shape in which to enjoy yoga's great gift of RELAXATION and SUPPORT.

One begins with lying down on one's back, preferably with a large bolster underneath to expand the chest. The soles of the feet meet on the ground like hands in prayer, and the knees diamond out to the sides. Straps and blocks are used to achieve both greater ease and greater opening.

A pose is classified as "Restorative" not just because of its energetic benefits, but because it involves the use of props, in this case, a bolster, straps, and blocks. Preparation is always required, meaning that things have to be set up in advance before the pose begins. By setting ourselves up properly with props, two powerful forces—Gravity and Time—now do all the work. In exactly the same way, we want to be set up properly in our financial lives for retirement.

Of course, some people choose never to retire, often out of passion for their work. The classic examples are often artists. Michelangelo and Titian did some of their finest work in old age; Lucian Freud painted up to his death at 88 in 2011, the same year the Louvre unveiled a 3,750 square foot commission from 83-year-old Cy Twombly. By the same token, 84-year-old financier George Soros (net worth $24.2 billion) announced his retirement recently for the second time, declaring "This time it's final!" —but only because he wants to devote more time to political philanthropy.

What's important, however, is working towards a reality where retirement choices are made out of desire and NOT financial necessity. That's why the uniqueness of each person's employment and financial situation again comes into play. Some careers might offer "golden parachutes" at retirement, whereas those in more maverick occupations will be well served knowing the ins and outs of setting up a Roth IRA (Individual Retirement Account) decades in advance.

We want to be sure retirement is not an unexpected problem we suddenly face later in life, a "surprise" forty years in the making. It's vital that we prepare all our "financial props" beforehand—our IRAs and Pensions, Medicare and Social Security—so that we can actually allow ourselves to relax into this period of our lives. Although we may not need $24 billion, like George Soros, we want to be in such a healthy financial situation that we can devote ourselves to whatever our true passions may be.

Of course, we can never know how long our retirement (or our non-retiring golden years) will last, but the hope is that they will be sustained for a long while. In the same way, restorative poses are designed to be held for more extended periods of time than other poses in their practice. In class, I might have students stay in Warrior Two for five breaths (about 30 seconds) before moving into another shape, but I budget three to five minutes per Restorative Pose, even longer with more experienced students.

We've reached a point in the Physical Practice where one no longer needs to expend large amounts of energy to achieve significant results. Just as Restorative Poses offer an often surprisingly vigorous amount of opening despite their stillness and seemingly passive appearance, we want retirement to also be a period of increased sense of freedom, new curiosity, and fresh adventures. Without falling into a cliché, we want those "golden years" to enjoy the same blend of ease and expansion.

We do not, however, in any way want to fall into a common trap of postponing happiness until age 65. Unfortunately, the mindset of "I'll work like a dog for 45 years and then take it easy for a decade or so before dying" still runs through much of our culture.

That's why a "Suffer Now/Relax on a Beach Later" mindset reflects perfectly the contrast between Problem Solving and Practice. Problem Solving is directed towards future happiness, whereas Practice is about happiness now AND later.

Knowing that the present is the only moment we truly ever have, in Practice Mode there's no conflict between our present day joy and setting up for a future full of further ease and flow.

INVITATIONS TO PRACTICE: MIND, BODY, and BANK ACCOUNT

Mind

Many of us often resist Support even when we deeply need it.

For example, do you feel you have to do everything for yourself? Are there areas where you could be more receptive to the help of others around you? Are you taking on too much or not asking for what you most desire?

Most importantly, are you taking care of your own needs first, or do you let those fall by the wayside in your service to others?

Uncover any resistance you have around being supported, as always being vigorous yet compassionate during your inquiry.

Body

Goddess pose or any other restorative shape is an ideal way to practice being supported and allowing opening to take place without exerting extra effort. In fact, often the most effective practice is a gentler, slower one.

Sometimes students who are quite comfortable with a flowing series of challenge poses find that resting in a sustained shape is unnerving. They simply cannot sit still in a pose without feeling the need to "do something." Can you allow yourself the luxury of relaxation and letting go, or do you always need to be forging ahead?

Finally, I encourage you to explore the benefits of restorative poses in isolation but also combined as part of a more dynamic, energetic practice. After warming the body up sufficiently through movement and breath, inhabiting a restorative shape like Goddess Pose offers tremendous opening potential.

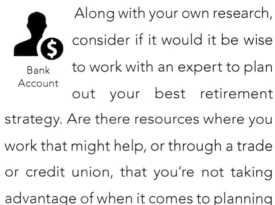 Along with your own research, consider if it would it be wise to work with an expert to plan out your best retirement strategy. Are there resources where you work that might help, or through a trade or credit union, that you're not taking advantage of when it comes to planning for your future?

Bank Account

Beyond this, consider other financial structures that could also serve to support your money goals.

For example, are there automatic savings plans offered at work or by your bank? What improved record-keeping or accounting strategies might serve you? Would switching to a discounted yearly payment or setting monthly ones up as auto-deductions simplify your financial life?

Uncover what allies—both individual and institutional—you can enlist to help support your present money moment and your future goals.

CHAPTER 10

MINDFULNESS

ALTERNATE NOSTRIL BREATHING

"Calming the mind is yoga, not just standing on the head."
~ Swami Satchidananda

THE BREATH •
MINDFUL PARTNERSHIPS

The breath is central to the entire practice of yoga, most importantly because attention to its ebb and flow is the cornerstone of MINDFULNESS.

No beginning student ever really believes me—I know I didn't really believe it years ago myself—that the most powerful way to adjust any pose is by watching the breath. Just yesterday, a new private student said to me, "I'll get the physical stuff down right and then I'll work on the breath." Unfortunately, he has it entirely in reverse. As soon as we become aware of the breath, it immediately shifts and deepens, and the body follows suit.

Almost everyone in our society is a habitually shallow breather, taking in just enough sips of air to survive. In the same way, over one-third of Americans live paycheck to paycheck, continually just getting by. Few of us take advantage of the fact that the breath is both the best barometer of our experience and the most powerful tool we have for Transformation.

That's because in yoga, breathing is more than just inhaling oxygen and nitrogen and exhaling them with a little more carbon dioxide thrown in the mix. Breathing means you're allowing *Prana* to flow through you.

Prana is defined as "life force," one that animates every cell in the body and everything in the universe. Look no further than Obi-Wan Kenobi's *Star Wars* definition of The Force: "It's an energy field created by all living things. It surrounds us and penetrates us; it binds the galaxy together." Depending on how corporate the environment I'm teaching in is, I'll share this explicitly or not, but its truth informs everything I offer in class.

Alternate nostril breathing is my favorite of the *Pranayamas* (meaning "breath stretching") practices because its effects are so powerful and centering. The right hand floats towards the face. The thumb blocks the right nostril and one exhales through the left, pauses when empty, and then inhales. With each exhale one switches sides, using either the thumb or the fourth and fifth fingers to block.

Yogis believe that this practice evens out the hemispheres of the brain, allowing one to feel more centered and calmer, even after only a few minutes. Just enough attention is required that one can stay focused but also serenely drift off, fully engaged with the simplicity of breathing in and out. Just watching the wave of breath creates Mindfulness.

In our financial practices, just as in our breathing, we also experience an endless cycle of ebb and flow. We exchange dollars for goods and services. We receive paychecks and we pay out expenses. Every balance sheet has both Assets and Liabilities. And on a grander level, the financial markets themselves fluctuate between bear and bullish cycles. This endless wave of financial and physical inhale/ exhale is a pattern that extends to everything in the Universe. Yet perhaps in our own lives, nothing rides the financial and emotional wave of ups and downs more dramatically than in our personal relationships.

The give and take between individuals—whether friends, business partners, or spouses—can result in our greatest joys and most painful heartaches. That's why Mindfulness—the gentle effort to be continuously present with those ever-changing experiences, no matter the highs or lows—is vital to any yoga or financial practice.

Earlier I quoted Thich Nhat Hanh: "No Mud, No Lotus." The lotus is a central theme and image in the yoga practice, demonstrating how CONTRAST—any element of our experience we dislike—not only is never going to go away, but it's also perhaps our greatest tool for growth.

We're never going to pretend that we like Contrast, or as Abraham says, "Put a smiley face sticker over an empty gas tank." That not only doesn't solve the problem, like Ostrich Pose, but living in denial also makes things much worse. Instead we're going to cultivate Mindfulness, the gentle effort to be continuously present with those ever-changing experiences, balancing out the highs or lows, the joys and the challenges.

Since the only constant in life is change, Mindfulness is vital to any yoga or financial practice. We absolutely must practice this on the mat and at the bank, but also in our personal relationships with friends, business partners, and spouses.

Mindful partnerships are those in which we practice the tools that yoga offers, particularly the benefits of a steady mind that comes from developing an awareness of our breath. Rather than instantly reacting (or over-reacting) in the heat of the moment, we don't repress our feelings but rather learn to allow them to pass like waves in the ocean. As Buddhist master Pema Chödrön says, "You are the sky. Everything else—it's just the weather." We work to cultivate the perspective of "The Witness," rather than indulging in the

"Monkey Mind" that merely instinctively reacts to stimuli.

Mindfulness allows us to have a broader sense of ourselves and that in turn gives us the space to be more compassionate with our intimates. We see ourselves from a steadier place, and from that broader perspective we can more skillfully navigate our dealings with the people in our lives. Rather than assigning blame or projecting our own fears and insecurities in our relationships, through mindfulness we practice staying in the present moment with our partners to create mutually satisfying solutions to our challenges, financial and otherwise.

Indeed, Money affects almost every relationship. Fighting about money remains the number one predictor of divorce, perhaps because couples often do not achieve a shared mindfulness about how they choose to approach their finances. This dialogue is vital yet often remains unspoken.

In the same way, in a modern world where nearly half of marriages end in divorce, how does one best come to terms with a fair pre- or post-nuptial agreement? How do you stay mindful enough to balance the blind optimism of romance with practical realities? And alongside romantic relationships, mindfulness is equally required when creating business partnerships (which also may not endure forever), or even when loaning money to friends and family.

Knowing that the breath is our greatest tool to regain our composure, settle our thoughts, and appreciate all our options, we can tune into Mindfulness simply by giving it our attention. Fortunately, our Yoga and Financial practices compliment each other as we seek out a centered awareness in all aspects of our personal and financial lives.

INVITATIONS TO PRACTICE: MIND, BODY, and BANK ACCOUNT

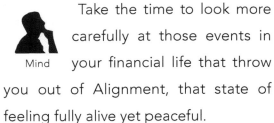

Mind

Take the time to look more carefully at those events in your financial life that throw you out of Alignment, that state of feeling fully alive yet peaceful.

Examine not only the immediate causes of your departure from feeling good but also the underlying beliefs that can make your thoughts turn negative and unfriendly.

In other words, can you move beyond the superficial source of your anxiety (an unexpected bill; a decrease in overtime hours) to the deeper root cause (doubts about the future; not asking for what you're really worth in salary)?

As always, try not to harshly judge the parts of your experience you dislike, but view everything as a vehicle for growth and part of your *YOGA OF* MONEY Practice.

Alternate Nostril Breathing has an incredible power to draw our attention inward and still our troubled minds.

Body

This ability to rapidly transform us from a tangled jumble of assortment of thoughts and conflicting emotions into a clearheaded and emotionally-centered person is invaluable, particularly when it comes to our interpersonal relationships. When navigating our way through emotional powder kegs, nothing could be more useful or strategic.

Examine all the partnerships that are part of your financial life, making to be sure that they are healthy and serving

Bank Account

both parties. This includes not only the most overt financial relationships (accountants, investment advisors, and business partners), but also personal relationships ranging from roommates to spouses where money comes into play.

Are you clearly communicating back and forth with each other? How might you improve the conversation?

Are partnership agreements in place wherever they are needed, whether these are formal documents drafted by attorneys or letters of agreement that you've created yourself?

An axiom often attributed to Einstein is that "Everything should be made as simple as possible, but not simpler." In all your partnerships, make sure things are as clear and as defined as they need to be for all parties to thrive.

CHAPTER 11

SURRENDER

CORPSE POSE

"Surrender is the highest power to gain
all that you want to gain."
~ Yogi Bhajan

CORPSE POSE •
LETTING GO & WHAT WE LEAVE BEHIND

A yoga practice always ends with Corpse Pose where we fully embody the concepts of SURRENDER and LETTING GO.

It's deceptively simple. One lies down, eyes closed, arms close to the sides, and palms open. After twisting and turning, going upside down, opening the heart center and the hips, and stretching in every way possible, for approximately five to ten minutes or so of stillness, the body is allowed to relax and absorb all the physical benefits of the class.

I enjoy the conceit that, on a physiological level, the body, like my laptop, needs and appreciates a reboot. As with any software update, the system will reset itself with newer, more open and flexible upgrades, but for that to happen, it must be momentarily shut down and then restarted.

Beyond the physical benefits for Corpse Pose, there are even more important symbolic reasons why we complete class this way. We are, first and foremost, reminded of our own mortality. Fully alive, we act out the role of a corpse, a particularly powerful contrast to the lively and dramatic way we have been moving previously. We simply practice being absolutely still. That's why, in Corpse Pose, the great lesson is Surrender.

Given that the yoga practice involves so many outrageous and difficult poses, it's ironic that Corpse Pose—just lying still for ten minutes—is often said to be the most challenging pose of all. B.K.S. Iyengar himself concludes that, "It is much harder to keep the mind than the body still. Therefore, this apparently easy posture is one of the most difficult to master." I've found this to be completely true in my own experience as a teacher. A significant portion of Type-A NYC personalities would rather be directed into a series of increasingly demanding physical activities than be invited to simply lie down and relax for five minutes.

Surrender can also be the most challenging part of our Financial Practice as well, both throughout our entire lives and in our legacies.

We can take the wisest and most strategic course of action as a matter of habit, but ultimately we have to let go again and again. We simply cannot control the flow of the stock market or the economy in general, and in our own lives not even our Christmas bonus or next promotion. Years ago, I'll never forget waiting impatiently around my mailbox for a promised royalty check (a very significant one), only to learn the distributor had gone bankrupt and that that check would never arrive. Surrender helps remind us that there truly is no such thing as a sure thing.

To really let go requires a degree of maturity that allows us to accept the fundamental truth of Impermanence: nothing lasts forever. As Pema Chödrön writes, "The root of suffering is resisting the certainty that no matter what the circumstances, uncertainty is all we truly have." Denial of this is why many people often avoid having a will or managing the legacy they will leave behind.

In Yoga Practice we gently confront the reality of mortality in every class. We are able to do so because we've continually reinforced the eternal nature of our soul, of our connection to the Divine, or however we choose to phrase it. In fact, we don't use words at all—we simply act out the mortality/eternalness paradox on our mats, knowing that the physical practice demonstrates things better than language ever could.

In the same way, making a will—a compassionate and sensible allocation plan for our assets after our deaths—allows us to not only surrender to the inevitable impermanence of our physical lives, but also to reconnect with the ongoing thread of existence. In other words, tending to our affairs in this way affirms that indeed "Life Goes On" after us.

Wisely and compassionately structuring our estate can be a final act of compassion that benefits generations to come. Being negligent and not doing so—or worse, trying to "settle scores" and have the last word—can be tremendously destructive. I've witnessed both applications.

Since we're practicing letting go in Corpse Pose, we're demonstrating an implicit faith in the ultimate wellbeing of the Universe, that our natural state is one of balance and alignment. That is indeed why Surrender is invaluable; we're reconnecting with our own eternal nature. Doing so, we learn that not only can we afford to let go, but also that the reward for doing so is priceless.

INVITATIONS TO PRACTICE: MIND, BODY, and BANK ACCOUNT

Mind

First, remember times in the past where you successfully experienced Letting Go, whether that involved physical objects you released or stories from the past that no longer served you. Recall moments of freedom and lightness you felt as you released something (or someone) and trust the lessons gleaned from those memories.

Next, let's examine the reality of our own mortality, fully aware that contemplating death often leads some into despondency or depression. On the other hand, as Ray Kurzweil writes, "Death gives meaning to our lives. It gives importance and value to time. Time would become meaningless if there were too much of it."

Contemplate the pragmatic optimism of this statement and the value, richness, and meaning of your own life. In particular, recognize all those who have touched your life and whose lives you have touched.

Corpse Pose is the perfect embodiment of the concepts of Letting Go and Surrender. Definitely incorporate it at the end of your physical yoga practice, but also explore how it might be included throughout. A two minute Savasana after a particularly challenging pose might allow the body to more fully absorb the wealth of benefits the Practice offers.

Body

Beyond the standard form of Corpse Pose—lying down, eyes closed, hands at one's side—see if you can also practice the FEELING of the shape in stressful situations. Can you "check out" of a difficult moment and "check in" with yourself before indulging in a knee-jerk reaction? Developing the ability to consciously Surrender could be a truly invaluable skill.

Bank Account

Do you have a will? Have you given any thought to how your affairs should be handled if you are incapacitated in any way? Remembering the lives that have touched you (and that you have touched), take pleasure in ways you can communicate that through your legacy.

After exploring all aspects of what arises in your Inner Life about surrendering to mortality, explore whether a standard internet available form is enough or whether the complexity of your estate requires hiring a good attorney to properly and compassionately manage what you leave behind.

CHAPTER 12

GRATITUDE

NAMASTE

"The attitude of gratitude is the highest yoga."

~ Yoga Bhajan

NAMASTE •
COMMUNITY & GIVING BACK

At the end of almost every yoga class, the teacher and students bring their hands into prayer. The teacher says, "*Namaste*" and the students echo this back, each bowing their head slightly forward towards the heart. *Namaste* acknowledges yet again that Yoga is not only a physical activity, but also a mental and spiritual Practice, one that gifts us with a reconnection to our community. Most importantly, we end every class with this beautiful expression of GRATITUDE.

This form of greeting and farewell originates in India. *Namaste* translates to "The Light within me honors the Light within you" or "The Divine in me honors the Divine in you." I have never attended a CrossFit class that ended in a similar salute to the Soul!

Namaste acknowledges that we are all connected in spirit, that we are all One. The idea of Separation is an illusion. As the Sufi mystic Rumi says: "Stop acting so small. You are the universe in ecstatic motion."

Just as OM frames our class, this final message of *Namaste* serves as a reminder that, although completely individual and distinct, we are interconnected and equal. We share a Divine Spark and we are part of a community—not just a local one but of humanity itself. Reconnected with that, we are now ready to re-enter the world.

Having emerged from Corpse Pose's reminder of our mortality, let's now address life's great other inevitability: Taxes.

Often the mere subject of taxes is enough to stir up all sorts of anxiety, resentment, and fear, usually destroying our peace of mind. Of course, as we look at our tax liabilities, we can absolutely apply the lessons of Focus by being strategic, consulting with experts, and making wise planning decisions throughout the year. More important though is our inner focus, practicing the fundamental first step of Acceptance and making peace with the requirements of our government that leads to Surrender. As always, *THE YOGA OF MONEY* helps us reframe these obligations from the perspective of our mind/body/spirit practice.

Taking this further, what would happen if we cultivated gratitude and appreciation around our taxes? Rather than resenting the government's perpetually having "its hand in our pockets," we might instead appreciate all that we receive but often take for granted in exchange for fulfilling our duties as law-abiding citizens. Paved roads, public schools, and libraries are shining examples of our tax dollars giving back to us. Even if we don't agree with how every penny of our tax dollars are being spent, we can take the broader view that so much of our lives and the lives of our communities are constantly enriched through this transfer of money. Ultimately, given our universal connection, everything we give, we only give back to ourselves.

Our final *Namaste* also underscores another level of connection and gratitude: the mutual respect and appreciation within the teacher/student relationship. The teacher bows first to his or her students (it is not a one-sided Guru/devotee relationship) and thanks the class for coming. The students bow back. Most students make a point of thanking their teacher as well when they exit, appreciating what's been shared together. With *Namaste* as a simple gesture of appreciation, we end every class powerfully by demonstrating the practice of Gratitude towards each other.

Another one of the best ways to celebrate the feeling of Gratitude is through Giving.

Giving is powerful, transforming both the giver and the receiver. I've often felt that perhaps the greatest joy of teaching for me is that I am giving the very best of myself and what I've learned. Frankly, teaching becomes an almost selfish act since not only do I receive so much back, I also most like being the person I am while teaching. The more I give my students, the more I receive.

In the same way, giving to others allows us to connect with the best part of ourselves: the capacity to be generous because we know that all is well, that we have more than enough to share, and that we are all connected. Giving lets us plug into a greater flow, a greater current of energy than we usually experience, one where fear and lack no longer have power over us.

There are, of course, infinite ways of giving, ranging from traditional tithing (giving 10% of one's earnings to a religious organization) to volunteering our time and talents. Perhaps the most important aspect of giving back is that it should happen NOW, not in some vague future moment when we imagine having a surplus of cash and time on our hands. You don't need to wait until you can finance a new wing to a hospital or endow a chair at a medical university; for only $50 you can give sight to a blind person through the Seva Foundation, for example, showing the astronomical benefit a relatively small amount of money can provide.

As we return more open physically to the world, with stretched spines, freer hips and looser hamstrings, most importantly we are centered within ourselves, more deeply connected to who we really are inside. *Namaste* signals that our time in the yoga studio may be complete for this particular day, but as is the nature of Practice, these lessons will extend and deepen into the rest of our lives. *Namaste* reminds us that as sparks of the Divine, we can and must reach out and give back to our community with greater generosity and an ever-expanding heart.

INVITATIONS TO PRACTICE: MIND, BODY, and BANK ACCOUNT

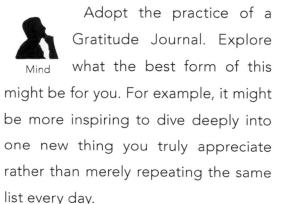

Mind

Adopt the practice of a Gratitude Journal. Explore what the best form of this might be for you. For example, it might be more inspiring to dive deeply into one new thing you truly appreciate rather than merely repeating the same list every day.

Remember that whatever we focus on expands. Therefore nothing could be more practical than to put the majority of our attention on the positive aspects of our life that we already enjoy.

Body

Practice the concept of "Namaste" by thanking more people in your life, particularly those you might take for granted. Note: this does not have to be elaborate. It might just be a sincere smile for your loved one loading the dishwasher, or a moment of appreciation of the person taking your ticket at the movie theater or the clerk at the DMV.

You might also cultivate the physical feeling of Gratitude in the body through experiences designed to enhance your sense of Appreciation. Taking long walks in nature, dancing to your favorite music, or indulging in a hot bath can provide a perfect focus for this kind of body-oriented Gratitude Meditation.

Bank Account

Can you feel Gratitude around your taxes? What stands in the way? How can you find peace regarding your relationship with the I.R.S.?

Beyond this, examine how you are giving in all areas of your life.

Are you contributing regularly to charity or to a spiritual source? Do you give freely to your friends and family or are you more inclined simply to receive unless asked directly?

Just as importantly, are there other ways you could give back besides money?

Check in with your Inner Guru about ways, both financially and with your time and talents, that you can give back more generously to both those closest to you and to the world beyond.

THE ETERNAL APPENDIX

One of the remarkable things about yoga practice, whether on the mat or in our financial lives, is that it's a never-ending adventure. There's always more to learn, always more to explore.

Many more resources—including FREE audio meditations and videos—are constantly being added to my website: www.EdwardVilga.com. Please visit so we can continue our yoga adventures together.

Remember: the journey lasts a lifetime.

Truly, your *YOGA OF MONEY* practice has just begun.

ACKNOWLEDGEMENTS

Since this book concludes with an entire chapter about Gratitude, it's only fitting that I practice what I preach and acknowledge as many people as I can who have been a part of this ongoing and dynamic *YOGA OF MONEY* journey.

First, I must thank my amazing literary agent Beth Vesel for not only her invaluable faith in and support of this project but also her brilliant and rigorous contribution to its development. Thank you, Beth.

It has also always been a great delight to work with my publicist Gail Parenteau on this and other projects.

I am also particularly grateful to Joshua Home Edwards who has been a true champion of *THE YOGA OF MONEY* from the moment it crossed his path.

Several generous friends read various drafts, offering insight (along with some good old-fashioned proofing): Jody Baron, Rita Durant, Hillary Kelleher, and Valerie Ross. I'd also like to thank Sue Peterson for weeding out the last round of typos and Alfredo Sarraga for artful design.

This material was developed through dozens of interviews, workshops, mastermind groups, a Daily OM online course, creative consultations and some guest teaching experiences. I appreciate everyone who participated, but I'd like to thank in particular Elizabeth Preston, Elaine Springer, Janet Bardini, Jessica Harrington, Leslie Jensen, Cha Cha Lopez, Amrita Nandakumar, Adrian Pineiro, Paula Krzystan, Lynette Lindahl, Rachel Saydak, Barbara Dixon, Cheryl Bailer, Simone and Fehmi Zeko, and Tamar Frumkin.

I'd like to acknowledge my great appreciation for Susan Kennedy and Scott Mills for offering me my first Guest Teaching gig.

Thank you, Stefanie Eris and Elizabeth Halfpapp, for your personal support of this work and for extending the lovely Exhale Mind Body Spa in NYC for workshops where it's my great pleasure to teach.

For the DAILY OM Course, I'd like to thank my gorgeous models: Leslie Lewis, Joe Mascali, Tammy Rowe, and Elaine Springer (and my chocolate lab, Belle!). I'd also like to thank Deonesea La Fey, my Author Liaison, for her support and enthusiasm; David Buchs for his lovely meditation music; Rick Mowat for his terrific cinematography; and my incredible Tech Wizard, Evan Mays, for behind the scenes magic.

For my own experiences of money in this world, I'd like to thank everyone with whom I've exchanged some kind of significant financial transaction. This list is vast, of course, but includes all my employers and all my private students and everyone who's invested in any of my projects.

I'd like to thank in particular anyone who lent me rent money, picked up a check, hosted me or offered some couch surfing, or sent me a surprise cash gift somewhere along the way: Amy Adler, Amy Ahlers, Jody Baron, Nicole Bettauer, Douglass Boyce, Cristy Candler, Sezin Cavusoglu, Bryn Chrisman, Gro Christensen, Nicky Dawda, Jude English, Dana Flynn, Roger Gonzalez, Sarah Herrington, Freddy Kaufman, Hillary Kelleher, Patty Kelly, Susan Kennedy, Carol Krenicky, Peter Lindy, Leslie Lewis, Genevieve Lynch, Natalie and Tony Moody, Melissa Morbeck, Dan Miller, Adrienne Opalka and Bert Orlov, Peter Phleger, Mary Sue Price, Jane Russell, Eva Saks. Ashleigh Young Santamaria, Daniel Scranton, Kathy Soroka, Jasmine Tarkeshi, Alex Tavis, Tim Tompkins, Tevis Trower, Haley Venn, Genevieve Vilga, and Helen Vilga.

When it comes to my yoga practice and career, my thanks could indeed be endless, particularly to my students. I would be remiss, however, not to mention my main teachers ranging from Dana Trixie Flynn to Sister Mary Alice who taught my first yoga class in junior high. I'd also like to mention Jasmine Tarkeshi and Jon Cassotta for their valuable roles in my development as student and teacher.

In terms of inspiration as well, there are countless people to thank, but I have to say that John Yuill's Human Design readings for me have refined and reinforced my sense of purpose more than I can say. I'd also like to thank Frank Butterfield for his wisdom along the way and Sarah Tomlinson for her beautiful yantra gift.

As a watery, homebody Cancerian, I'm extremely grateful to the entire staff, my neighbors and the community of my building in NYC, in particular to the extraordinary Leslie Lewis for making my life here possible.

From somewhere in the Vortex, I'd also like to think that my Dad, Genevieve Vilga, John Waddell,

Robin Mookerjee, and Natalie Moody have been extending some deeply appreciative non-physical guidance.

Finally, as always, I'd like to thank NW for her early encouragement of my yoga teaching career, as well as my beloved MT's enthusiasm for my online course launch.

• Om Shreem Hreem Saraswatyai Namaha •

AUTHOR BIO

"What Karl Lagerfeld is to fashion, Edward Vilga is to yoga."

Simon Doonan • Author, legendary fashionista, and Barneys' Creative Ambassador

Edward Vilga has taught yoga throughout New York City—including on the jumbotron in Times Square—and around the world for nearly 20 years.

He is also the author of eight published books, including the bestselling YOGA IN BED.

That book and DVD have been featured in PEOPLE and Oprah's O MAGAZINE, along with TV shows such as LIVE WITH KELLY, CBS' EARLY SHOW, and over 50 other publications. YOGA IN BED has been translated into more than a dozen languages.

Edward Vilga is a Yale graduate.

Most importantly, he is rarely seen without his chocolate lab, Belle.

You're cordially invited to visit www.EdwardVilga.com for more information, along with free audio meditations and yoga videos.

69273220R00102

Made in the USA
Middletown, DE
05 April 2018